Self-Esteem Games for Children

Deborah M. Plummer

Illustrations by Jane Serrurier

Jessica Kingsley Publishers
London and Philadelphia

First published in 2007
by Jessica Kingsley Publishers
116 Pentonville Road
London N1 9JB, UK
and
400 Market Street, Suite 400
Philadelphia, PA 19106, USA

www.jkp.com

Copyright © Deborah M. Plummer 2007
Illustrations copyright © Jane Serrurier 2007
Printed digitally since 2011

Library of Congress Cataloging in Publication Data
Plummer, Deborah.
  Self-esteem games for children / Deborah M. Plummer ; illustrations by Jane Serrurier.
     p. cm.
  Includes bibliographical references and index.
  ISBN-13: 978-1-84310-424-7 (pbk.)
  ISBN-10: 1-84310-424-5 (pbk.)
  1. Self-esteem in children. 2. Self-esteem in children--Problems, exercises, etc. I. Title.
  BF723.S3P59 2007
  155.4'182--dc22

                                                        2006034312

British Library Cataloguing in Publication Data
A CIP catalogue record for this book is available from the British Library

ISBN 978 1 84310 424 7
eISBN 978 1 84642 574 5

Contents

Part One: Theoretical and practical background

Part Two: Games for self-esteem

List of games

Part One

Theoretical and practical background

1

Introduction

The imperative for combining theory with practice

Picture the following imaginary scenario. Seven-year-old Adam is joining in with a group game of 'By the sea' – an active, fun game chosen by group facilitator Maggie to help the children to let off steam. The group has previously been concentrating on a written task which proved to be quite difficult for Adam. 'You're already OUT Adam!' comes the indignant cry from Ben. 'You can't keep joining in when you're ALREADY OUT!' Maggie invites Adam to stand near her and help her to decide who is out next time. Adam reluctantly agrees but during the next round insists that Ben is 'out'. The game quickly deteriorates into a series of denials and second chances. Finally an exhausted Maggie brings things to an early close when she spots Adam systematically emptying out the contents of the sand tray in the far corner of the room.

Why is it that some group games seem to 'work' and others don't? I believe that one of the main reasons lies in how well the facilitator understands the importance of the game process and how powerful this process can be. Of course, games played as energizers or treats can be exciting and fun and a source of immense pleasure for the players. Occasionally, however, they can also be sheer torture for the quiet child, the child who has difficulty understanding the rules of games, the child who is already full of pent-up frustration or anxiety, or who fears being 'left out' or losing yet again. In contrast, a well-chosen game played with awareness on the part of the facilitator can be an incredibly effective instrument for supporting a child's emergent sense of self and self-esteem.

Without this awareness the many opportunities for helping children to build cognitive, social and emotional skills through the medium of games can so easily be missed or, worse still, can unwittingly be misused and foster even deeper feelings of low self-worth.

My aim in writing this handbook is therefore to facilitate a mindful approach to playing self-esteem games by bringing together some of the theory of self-esteem and of play and combining this with guidelines for playing a range of non-competitive games. These are intended to supplement other strategies that facilitators are already using in order to contribute to an *integrated approach* to help 5–11-year-olds build, maintain and reinforce healthy self-esteem. Games alone are not the panacea for all self-esteem ills and, realistically, 'Maggie' and I are not super-enlightened, constantly mindful people, but in recognizing the nature and power of games we can certainly give it all we've got!

I have chosen to focus on non-competitive games where the enjoyment and the challenge come from the process itself rather than from winning. This is not because I have an aversion to competitive games. In fact, far from this being the case, I do believe that there is a place for such games once a child is ready to engage in them and does so by their own choice. The child's world is after all a competitive arena and most children will naturally play games of skill that involve winning or losing or being 'in' or 'out' whether we adults encourage them or not. Younger children and those who are particularly vulnerable to low self-esteem will find these win-or-lose games extremely difficult to cope with, however, and will need to first develop a certain degree of emotional resilience, competence and self-efficacy, all of which can be fostered initially through non-competitive activities.

During my years as a speech and language therapist I have collected many different games from various sources. Some of them have been passed on to me by colleagues in the teaching and therapy professions or by children in therapy groups; some came from books; many are adaptations of school and party games I remember playing as a child; some are games that I have played on various professional training courses. Occasionally, when I believe that I have made up an entirely new game to suit therapy purposes, I later come across just such a game being used in a different context! Such is the nature of games – because they follow certain conventions they are constantly being recycled and re-invented in playgrounds, therapy rooms, classrooms and homes across the world.

The games presented here have been selected on the basis of clinical experience and observations to represent just a few of the many possibilities. It will quickly become apparent that throughout the sections there are also a handful of activities that are not structured games in the true sense of the word but do involve an element of play. These have been added because I have found them to be particularly helpful tools in the self-esteem tool box. The stretching of a definition to encompass these activities is, I hope, a useful transgression! Further similar activities can also be found in *Helping Children to Build Self-Esteem* (Plummer 2001).

With occasional adaptations, all the games can be played in schools and will fit into a wide selection of personal, social and health education (PSHE) and other learning objectives. The material can also be incorporated into a diverse range of therapy approaches with individual children or groups.

Crucially, many of the games can be played at home by families. The role played by parents and siblings in supporting a child's self-esteem is tremendously important, and encouraging families to play these games together can have a far-reaching impact on the process. The special time shared between family members during a fun game can, in itself, be a boost to helping parents to understand their children, show their love, and strengthen their relationship. In the context of self-esteem, sharing moments of laughter, problem-solving and creativity during games can be rewarding and re-affirming for both children and parents.

However, for families who do not generally play games together the idea of incorporating game activities into their daily lives can be extremely daunting. Encouraging parents to play games as part of a therapeutic or teaching strategy needs to be approached very carefully and with full awareness of how easy it is for adults to misconstrue the reasons for playing games. 'Keep it simple, keep it fun' is the best guideline.

I have not attempted to offer any formula for choosing which games to play or how many to play at any one time. This is because the ways in which the games are adapted and incorporated into educational and therapy approaches can and should vary according to the setting and according to the needs, strengths and experiences of the children. Each facilitator will naturally bring their own personality, imagination, expertise and knowledge to the games and create something new from the basic format. In this way, playing with the process of playing becomes an integral part of our own learning.

How to use this book

The games and activities are divided into nine sections: warm-ups, the seven foundation elements of healthy self-esteem (Plummer 2001) and wind-downs.

In some instances this categorization is slightly arbitrary since many of the games could be placed in more than one section. Because the elements of self-esteem are intimately connected, you will find that you are often touching on several aspects within just one game. However, if you keep the principal focus in mind this will help you to evaluate and adapt individual games appropriately.

Each section starts with a brief overview of the process or the foundation element to be explored. This is followed by a selection of games relevant to that particular aspect.

As well as the primary objective, you will also find a list of additional skills that each game could promote. I have chosen to limit these lists to just a few key areas but there is plenty of room for you to add further skills that you feel are important for your own focus of work. Undoubtedly, the more often that you play these games, the more skills you will want to add to each list!

For ease of reference, the games have been marked with a set of symbols to indicate age-appropriateness and the amount of speaking involved. The symbols used are as follows:

⑤	This gives an indication of the suggested *youngest* age for playing the game. There is no upper age limit.
⏲ 10 mins	An approximate time is given for the length of the game (excluding the discussion time). This will obviously vary according to the size of group and the ability of the players.
♦ ♦ ♦	Indicates that the game is suitable for larger groups (eight or more).
♦ ♦	The game is suitable for small groups.
♡♡♡	The game involves a lot of speaking unless it is adapted.
♡♡	A moderate amount of speaking is required by players.
♡	The game is primarily a non-verbal game or one requiring minimal speech.
☑ observation	This gives an indication of an additional key skill used or developed by playing this game.

Language levels

Although the amount of speaking involved in each game has been noted, the games have not been categorized according to levels of verbal understanding nor according to the spoken language *ability* needed. Some games will obviously require adaptations to support children with specific speech and language difficulties or learning difficulties. You may find that children who do not have the necessary understanding of more complex verbal instructions may just need time to observe others before joining in or they may benefit from having the instructions broken down into smaller chunks. It will be important to then check their understanding after each part of the instruction.

Adaptations

Ideas for expanding and adapting the games are offered as a starting point for your own experimentation with the main themes.

Reflection

Each game description finishes with a selection of ideas for reflection and for discussion with older children. These suggestions are also intended to provide focus points for facilitators to use during their own planning and reflection meetings.

Sometimes even the briefest time spent in reflecting on the process of a game can help children to realize that they are not alone in how they feel and this in itself can be a tremendously helpful experience for the child with low self-esteem. Equally, children who play games regularly will often learn purely through the experience and will not necessarily need to verbally reflect on what happened within the sessions. As a general principle I would suggest that we should not give more time to a discussion at the time of playing than we do to the game itself. It is the experience of the game that is the most important aspect. However, these topics can provide an opportunity for drawing links between different themes at later times. You could remind children of particular games when this is relevant: 'Do you remember when we played that game of "Pass the shell"? What did you feel when you were praised?'

Coordinator's notes

Although this is first and foremost a resource book, emphasis is also placed on the value of reflective practice. If we are to be effective in our work with children then we must, of course, continually evaluate and monitor our own skills and reflect on our personal learning. Each page therefore includes space for facilitators to add their own notes. These might include such things as personal insights and experiences of using the games, personal preferences, dislikes, problems and successes (see pages 30–31 for further guidelines).

Finally, because you will undoubtedly have many more games in your repertoire and will gather further ideas from colleagues and children, each section ends with a blank summary page for 'additional notes'. Here you can add to your list and make any further general comments on your experiences with the games you have used.

My hope is that this format will encourage reflective practice but that it will not *dis*courage enjoying the pure fun of playing games with young children. This, after all, is the essential value of self-esteem games – having fun while learning about ourselves and others!

The remainder of Part One explores the concept of self-esteem, outlines the significance of play in the development of feelings of self-worth and competence in young children and offers guidelines for facilitating the games.

2

Understanding self-esteem

The link between self-esteem and mental, physical and emotional well-being has long been recognized. Self-esteem is a thoroughly researched area, not least because of the well-documented interplay between personal feelings of self-worth and self-efficacy on the one hand and wider social concerns on the other. Educationalists such as Peter Gurney, for example, have argued that self-esteem is of central importance as a foundation for learning and therefore should be '*the* prime goal for education' (Gurney 1988) while the California Task Force to Promote Self-Esteem and Personal and Social Responsibility (1990) emphasized the possibility of low self-esteem being linked with such issues as teenage pregnancy and suicidal thoughts.

Self-concept and self-esteem

In order to understand self-esteem we need to also understand how psychologists define self-concept. R.B. Burns, for example, describes the self-concept as 'a composite image of what we think we are, what we think we can achieve, what we think others think of us and what we would like to be' (Burns 1979, p.vi). Developmental psychologist Susan Harter prefers the term 'self-representations', which she defines as 'attributes or characteristics of the self that are consciously acknowledged by the individual through language – that is, how one describes oneself' (Harter 1999, p.3).

In essence, then, our self-concept is the internal 'word' and 'picture' image that we have of ourselves at any given time. This image includes our physical characteristics and our abilities, attitudes and beliefs.

Our self-concept largely determines our behaviour – we will tend to act in ways that are consistent with our internal images (see pages 14–15).

In the early years of childhood our self-concept is very malleable and hugely dependent on the way in which we interpret the reactions or feedback from other people (the way we perceive their reactions to us and to what we do and say). Undoubtedly, the majority of us will continue to be affected to some degree by actual or perceived evaluations by others throughout our lives but, in general, as we get older we gradually develop the ability to make realistic self-assessments and rely less and less on these externally perceived judgements.

Such internal and external judgements also affect the images that we form of the 'ideal' self – the person whom we would like to be or think we should be – and the difference between the perceived self (self-concept) and the 'ideal' self gives some indication of levels of self-esteem. Someone with low self-esteem for example may create an unrealistic image of her ideal self so that the gap between how she has constructed her self-concept and the self she strives for appears insurmountably huge.

So, self-esteem is related to our evaluation of our self-concept. It is 'the relative degree of worthiness, or acceptability, which people perceive their self-concept to possess' (Gurney 1988, p.39) and it is inextricably tied up with our early life-experiences and the influence of the significant people in our lives.

During the late 1950s and early 1960s psychologist Stanley Coopersmith conducted extensive research in the area of self-esteem which he defined as 'the extent to which the individual believes himself to be capable, significant, successful and worthy. In short, self-esteem is a *personal* judgement of worthiness that is expressed in the attitudes the individual holds towards himself' (Coopersmith 1967, p.5). This definition applies to the estimation of *general* or 'global' self-esteem.

As Susan Harter points out, it is important to also distinguish between

> self-evaluations that represent global characteristics of the individual (e.g., 'I am a worthwhile person') and those that reflect the individual's sense of adequacy across particular domains such as one's cognitive competence (e.g., 'I am smart'), social competence (e.g., 'I am well liked by peers'), athletic competence (e.g., 'I am good at sports') and so forth. (Harter 1999, p.5)

Not all domains are equally as accessible or as abundant with regard to self-esteem, and levels of self-esteem in different domains may alter according to circumstances. Also, the extent to which self-evaluations in various domains affects our global sense of self-worth will depend partly on the level of importance we place on each one.

A self-esteem schema might then look something like the one outlined in Figure 2.1.

The self-evaluations of most young children usually involve descriptions of behaviours, abilities and preferences. They are often unrealistically positive and tend to involve polar opposites of good and bad, including good feelings (emotions) and bad feelings. Although this may be the general trend, research has increasingly shown that even very young children can demonstrate low self-esteem if their life experience has emphasized negative attributes (Harter 1999).

As Coopersmith (1967) and others have noted, natural shifts in self-evaluation can and do occur in different situations and at different times. These changes may be due to the type of task that we are attempting, our mood at the time or the prevailing attitude of the important people in our lives, and for the most part such changes are a normal aspect of healthy self-esteem. However, some people find these fluctuations much more difficult to cope with so that negative self-evaluations in specific domains quickly affect global self-esteem, as if the plug has been pulled on the entire 'self-esteem pot'.

Coopersmith's definition of self-esteem highlights another central element of self-esteem: that it is not just about self-evaluation or 'feeling good about ourselves'; most importantly, it is also about actual and perceived competence and what social learning theorist

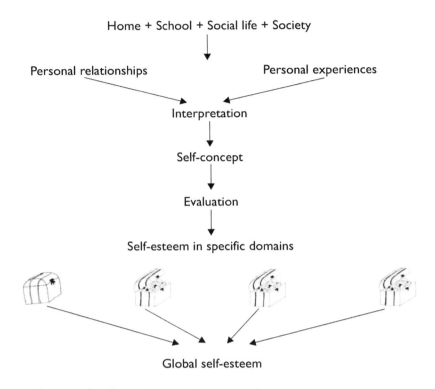

Home + School + Social life + Society

Personal relationships   Personal experiences

Interpretation

Self-concept

Evaluation

Self-esteem in specific domains

Global self-esteem

Figure 2.1 Global and specific self-esteem (Source: Plummer 2005)

Albert Bandura called self-efficacy – the belief that we are capable of doing something and that we can influence events that affect our lives (Bandura 1977).

In his exploration of the experiences associated with self-esteem, Coopersmith (1967) describes various hypothetical internal monologues or self-descriptive statements that might be used by people with different levels of self-esteem. In essence, this is the 'story' that we tell ourselves about who we are. And, of course, the story that we tell at any given time will affect how we feel, behave, learn and relate to other people. If I have particularly low self-esteem perhaps my internal monologue might go something like this: 'I'm rubbish. I can't do anything as well as the rest of the class. Nobody wants to be friends with me. Everyone thinks I'm stupid…'

Notice the 'all or nothing' nature of this self-talk – anything, nobody, everyone – and the fact that it is in the present tense. These two aspects give an all-pervading sense of hopelessness. I am also telling my story as if my perceptions and feelings are actual facts about 'who I am' and about what other people think. The story that I tell may well become my self-fulfilling prophecy because I am building images of myself as a 'rubbish, useless person that nobody likes'. These images in turn will inform the way that I relate to others, not just at the moment of telling myself the story but also in the future, because if I tell the story often enough the images will be imprinted in my subconscious. In this way, even if I have concepts of myself which are not consistent with reality, they are true for me because I *believe* them to be true.

Is it possible to change this pattern? Thankfully, yes. And I can do this in a number of ways. I can choose to bring some of my subconscious images to the surface and work with them in a constructive way (see for example Glouberman 2003; Hillman 2002; Johnson 1989; Plummer 1999, 2001, 2005); I can change my outward behaviour; or I can change the story that I tell myself (my thinking patterns). In fact, whichever approach I use, changes in one dimension will have repercussions in the others – it is not possible to change one aspect alone without influencing the others since they are all intimately connected.

So, for example, when I change the story that I tell myself, I gradually change the subconscious images that inform my behaviour and I begin to act in ways that are congruent with my new thoughts and beliefs.

The role of adults

When children have early life experiences which reinforce negative images, changing the current story may be a long, slow process. There may also be a marked time lag before the way that they behave with others 'catches up' with the new version of the internal story. In some instances, the reverse may be true – a child may learn to behave in certain ways in order to cover up their true sense of low self-worth and it is the feelings that have to catch up with the behaviour. This means that we cannot always rely on observable behaviour alone to give us an indication of levels of self-esteem. It also points to the fact that adults need to be aware of their vital role in helping children not only to *develop* self-esteem but also to *maintain* healthy self-esteem in the midst of life's challenges and inconsistencies. Self-esteem is not something that we are born with – it develops over time – and there is much that adults can do to encourage, enhance and reinforce this development, just as there is much that can be done to help a child to repair damaged self-esteem.

Coopersmith set out to answer the question 'What are the conditions that lead an individual to value himself and to regard himself as an object of worth?' He summarized the answers to this question as 'parental warmth', 'clearly defined limits', and 'respectful treatment', adding that these terms were 'more complex and ambiguous than generally appreciated' (Coopersmith 1967, p.vii).

In essence, children are most likely to have healthy self-esteem when the significant people in their lives are accepting and non-judgemental and when communication is clear and unambiguous. When children feel genuinely valued and respected as unique individuals then they are far more likely to value, respect and approve of themselves.

This is not just a psychological/emotional outcome of positive early experiences. There has been much research in recent years indicating that both positive and negative early interaction patterns can profoundly affect the long-term chemical balance and neural pathways of an infant's growing brain. Research neuroscientist Lise Eliot, for example, cites a study undertaken by researchers at the University of Washington who compared frontal-lobe EEG measures in the infants of depressed and non-depressed mothers. They found that by about one year of age, babies whose mothers were depressed showed a different pattern of neural responsiveness than control babies. During playful interactions, they experienced less activation of the left hemisphere (the 'feel-good' side) than control babies (Eliot 1999). It appears that in more extreme cases the physiological effects of neglect or lack of loving relationships during babyhood will severely complicate the recovery pattern of children with marked lack of self-esteem.

The need for awareness

In the wake of Coopersmith's research and several other major studies, the 1990s saw a huge growth in the publication of self-esteem textbooks and manuals. This rapid growth of the 'self-esteem' movement inevitably also brought with it what Christopher Mruk (1999) refers to as the self-esteem 'backlash' – claims by some professionals that emphasis on self-esteem is misleading and is obscuring other, more important aspects of child-development and child-rearing. Mruk points out that this backlash appears to have arisen because of a fundamental misunderstanding of what self-esteem is – a misguided belief that it relies almost totally on feeling good about oneself, possibly fostering a narcissistic tendency to the detriment of others. This is not, of course, what we are aiming for when we set out to support the development and maintenance of healthy self-esteem. In fact, many psychologists would argue that children and adults who show some of the features associated with being self-absorbed or narcissistic actually have *low* self-esteem and are therefore over-compensating in their attempts to feel better about themselves.

Such a dispute does, however, add significant emphasis to the need for approaching self-esteem concerns with *integrity* and *mindfulness*. In the context of facilitating games in a therapeutic or teaching environment, for example, we need to be fully aware of why we are playing the games that we have chosen; fully conscious of the possible effects that playing such games might have; and fully 'present' with the children in order to understand their ways of responding and interacting and to appreciate the spontaneous learning that is occurring within and between group members.

So, in helping a child to build and maintain healthy levels of self-esteem, we need to:

- be curious about his internal monologue (his theory about himself)
- show genuine warmth and respect for him as a unique individual
- be fully aware of how our actions and words affect his self-concept and therefore his levels of self-esteem
- help him to develop self-awareness and realization of how his behaviour affects other people
- help him to develop the ability to make realistic self-evaluations
- help him to understand that self-esteem can change in form and intensity according to many different factors and that this is normal, but that it need not have a negative effect on his overall sense of self and 'worthwhileness'.

The foundation elements for healthy self-esteem

Healthy self-esteem can be seen as having seven 'foundation elements' (Plummer 2001). These elements are outlined at the start of each of the relevant sets of games in Part Two. Although some areas may be more central to each child's feelings of self-worth and competence than others, I believe that it is important to explore all seven areas in order to help children to establish and maintain healthy self-esteem. The interaction is reciprocal – healthy levels of self-esteem will enable the consolidation and growth of these elements.

Assessing levels of self-esteem

Invariably when I run workshops on self-esteem one of the most frequently asked questions is 'How do we measure it?' This seems to have become even more of an issue in the light of the growing emphasis on evidence-based practice and measurable outcomes in many professions. Teachers and practitioners are increasingly looking for 'before and after' measures that can be used to indicate whether or not intervention methods have indeed resulted in children developing a stronger sense of self-esteem.

Whilst I appreciate the need for this question, it is not a straightforward one to answer! Self-esteem is, after all, a hypothetical construct and therefore by its very nature difficult to measure. We can measure behaviours that might occur as a *result* of different levels of feelings of self-worth or competency, but, as I have already suggested, behaviour may not always be a true reflection of feelings at any given time. Should we then rely on children reporting how they *feel* in different situations, or do we need a combination of assessments? The following brief outline of three of the available tools may help you to decide whether and how you will incorporate formal assessments for self-esteem into your work with children.

Amongst the earliest and most often used measures for children are the Rosenberg (1965) 'self-esteem scale' and the Coopersmith (1967) 'self-esteem inventory'.

Rosenberg's scale was devised to measure global feelings of self-worth and self-acceptance in adolescents. It includes ten items (such as 'I am able to do things as well as most other people') which are scored on a response range from 'strongly disagree' to 'strongly agree'. There is also a six-item format for children under 11 years old (Rosenberg and Simmons 1972). The scale offers an estimate of positive or negative feelings about the self and has found widespread popularity partly because of its ease of administration and scoring.

Coopersmith's original self-esteem inventory (SEI) was developed for research, as an assessment of children's attitudes towards themselves both generally and in specific contexts. There are eight items used for cross-checking the reliability of the children's responses and 50 statements which contribute to the overall score. These reflect self-attitudes in four areas: school, peers, parents and personal interests. For example, 'I often wish I were someone else', 'I'm a lot of fun to be with', 'my parents expect too much of me' and 'I find it very hard to talk in front of the class'. For each statement children choose the response 'like me' or 'unlike me'. Most of these statements were based on those developed by Carl Rogers and Rosalind Dymond (1954) and reworded for use with children aged eight to ten. One criticism of this scale has been that because it groups domain-specific self-evaluations into one final score it 'masks the meaningful distinctions between an individual's sense of adequacy across domains' (Harter 1999, p.5).

Coopersmith also devised a 13-item behaviour rating form (BRF) for teachers to complete. This looked at such things as the behaviour of children when faced with failure and their need for encouragement and reassurance.

Both the SEI and the BRF can be found in Coopersmith's book *The Antecedents of Self-Esteem* (1967), together with a thorough exploration of the theoretical aspects of his research. Psychologist and teacher Peter Gurney also outlines a revised 37-item format of the SEI and a revised ten-item BRF which he feels are particularly suited for use with children with special educational needs. Gurney describes the revised scale as 'the result of a research effort to rewrite Coopersmith's test items to make them suitable for English children and to produce adequate reliability and validity data' (Gurney 1988, p.39).

There are also many self-concept scales in existence, some of which include attempts at measuring self-esteem. Some of these measurements have been criticized as being conceptually difficult for young children to grasp and for not taking into account cultural and gender differences in how children view themselves in relation to others (Butler and Gasson 2005).

Richard Butler's self image profiles for children and adolescents (SIPs) are a welcome addition to the available assessment tools (Butler 2001). These profiles are based on the principles of personal construct theory proposed by George Kelly in the 1950s and 'the developmental and organisational aspects of self' proposed by Harter in the 1990s and are one of only a handful of British scales developed for self-esteem assessment. The profiles each consist of 25 items; 12 of these are positive in nature and 12 are negative. There is also one neutral item. Children and adolescents are invited to give two ratings for each item to indicate how they see themselves now and how they would like to be. The discrepancy between the two ratings is taken to be a measure of self-esteem.

Returning to mindfulness

While spending time researching the various scales and measurements in use, one thought consistently bothered me, or at least kept bringing me back to the imperative for working mindfully with the children in our care. This is that we should not forget that in undertaking an assessment of self-esteem in a therapeutic or teaching context we are by inference working with particularly vulnerable children. Asking a child to complete a rating scale may therefore in itself prove problematic. We should be aware that for some children this self-judgement might be seen as suggesting that self-esteem has an intrinsic worth; that we can have a 'right' or 'wrong' amount. Children may also be unrealistic in their self-ratings, try to give what they perceive to be 'acceptable' answers or scores, or they may find it difficult to link feelings in certain situations with how they actually behave.

Similarly, rating scales and questionnaires completed by observers or carers also risk the danger of becoming value-laden or judgemental in some way. At what level can we confidently say 'this score indicates a child with healthy levels of self-esteem' or 'this score indicates that a child will struggle to make friends'?

Whatever assessment is used, it is clear that it can only be truly useful if it is administered mindfully, is interpreted in the light of each child's individual nature and circumstances and is not seen as a measure of comparison with the abilities and achievements of other children.

Perhaps checklists of observable behaviour may be more valuable, not so much as a *measure* of self-esteem but as an indication of areas for concern. Peter Gurney provides a useful list of possible signs of low self-esteem in children aged 5 to 15 (Gurney 1988). The list includes 49 items covering personal behaviour, social behaviour and school work. Gurney makes the point that a child experiencing problems in just one of these areas may not necessarily have low self-esteem and that the checklist is not enough of an indicator on its own – it should be combined with talking to the child herself and to her parents/carers. He also comments that 'it is pointless to use this list until an adequate system of consultation and communication exists in the school and staff members have had some training in self-esteem enhancement strategies' (p.49). In other words, he believes that the value of such check-lists lies in how they will inform school policy rather than whether or not they have research validity. A short checklist can also be found in *Helping Children to Build Self-Esteem* (Plummer 2001).

In the long term, it is self-assessment that is of primary importance and, for the majority of children, this is a skill that can be learned and developed over time. It obviously takes a great deal of practice for children to be able to monitor and realistically assess their own behaviour and feelings. There is also a developmental perspective to consider. In order to make realistic self-evaluations children need to have reached certain cognitive milestones. These include the abilities to compare themselves with others; to make distinctions between actual and ideal self-concepts; to view things from different perspectives; and to understand the difference between effort and ability (Harter 1999). They need to understand, too, that it is possible to have fluctuations in how confident and competent they feel and that this is normal.

Adults can do much to support children as they negotiate this discovery of different aspects of the 'self', and one of the major ways in which we can do this is to encourage and support them in their play.

3

Why use games to support healthy self-esteem?

Play and 'playing games'

At our very earliest stages of development, play is how we find out about ourselves and the world: play through manipulation of our own body (e.g. sucking a thumb or toes); play with sounds (e.g. babbling); play with an object (e.g. a comfort blanket); play with a significant other (e.g. the 'mirroring' of facial expression and body movements that often occurs so naturally between a parent and child, games of peek-a-boo and waving 'bye bye'). In this way we gradually learn what is 'me' and 'not me', we learn the rudiments of cause and effect and turn-taking. We even learn to cope with feelings of temporary separation and loss with games such as hide-and-seek.

From this type of play we move on gradually to symbolic play – manipulation of objects as symbols of real things – and then to imaginary play, where some props may be used but much, or all, of the scenario is imagined: 'I'm the mummy and I have to feed the baby', 'I will be the princess and you can be the wicked witch' or 'I'm a policeman and I'm looking for a robber.'

By working our imagination like a muscle we learn to problem-solve, to work through some of life's difficulties, to reach our own 'child-level' of understanding of the complexities of the world – we make 'child-sense' of our experiences in a simplified and safe way and thereby strengthen our emotional resilience.

Play of one sort or another provides invaluable opportunities for children to experience the consequences of their actions and to experiment with different skills and different outcomes without fear of failure or being judged unfavourably by others. Play is also a medium through which children can expand and consolidate their language skills.

Psychologist Catherine Garvey suggests that

> because playing is voluntarily controlled (executed in a way in which imperfect achievement is minimally dangerous), its effects are probably intricately related to the child's mastery and integration of his experiences…when the behaviour is next performed in a non-play mode, it may be more skilled, better integrated, and associated with a richer or wider range of meaning. In this way play can contribute to the expertise of the player and to his effectiveness in the non-play world. (Garvey 1977, p.118)

Vivian Paley has also documented many crucial observations of the importance of children's play. As a nursery teacher she became increasingly aware of how children in her classes placed a great deal of emphasis on things that happened during play activities – it was the themes that arose during play that they were most likely to want to discuss. In her wonderful book *The Boy Who Would Be a Helicopter* Paley observes that children's rites and images in play

> seem mainly concerned with the uses of friendship and fantasy to avoid fear and loneliness and to establish a comfortable relationship with people and events. In play, the child says, 'I can *do* this well; I can *be* this effectively; I *understand* what is happening to me and to other children.' (Paley 1991, p.10)

How do games fit into this magical world of play? Garvey defines games as play activities that are structured with 'explicit rules that can be precisely communicated' (1977, p.101). The ability to play games with rules usually emerges at around five or six years of age although, as outlined above, the early signs of this can be seen with very young infants (a game of peek-a-boo for example involves structured turn-taking to some extent and children of three often understand the 'unspoken' rules of familiar games). By around five years of age children are more able to tolerate waiting and a degree of inevitable frustration at being 'out' in a competitive game. They are beginning to exercise self-control and the ability to follow rules and conventions. They are also more able to sustain interactions with others for longer periods.

Games generally have clear start and finishing points and follow sequences which are accepted by the players and which can therefore be replicated at other times and in different situations. In this way they provide a sense of predictability and security even when the game itself might be a bit scary!

> A true game is one that frees the spirit. It allows of no cares but those fictitious ones engendered by the game itself. When the players commit themselves to the rhythm and incident of 'Underground tig' or 'Witches in the gluepots' they opt out of the ordinary world, the boundary of their existence becomes the two pavements this side of a pillar box, their only reality the excitement of avoiding the chaser's touch. (Opie and Opie 1976, p.40)

Opie and Opie conducted extensive research into children's street games in the 1960s. They observed that

> children like games in which there is a sizeable element of luck, so that individual abilities cannot be directly compared. They like games which restart almost automatically, so that everybody is given a new chance. They like games which move in stages, in which each stage, the choosing of leaders, the picking-up of sides, the determining of which child shall start, is almost a game in itself…many of the games, particularly those of young children, are more akin to ceremonies than competitions. In these games children gain the reassurance that comes with repetition, and the feeling of fellowship that comes from doing the same as everyone else. (pp.40–41)

In their daily lives children constantly have to negotiate their way through a welter of adult-imposed rules, structures and boundaries. Sometimes these are explicit but often they are unclear or unspoken, taken for granted. Rules for games on the other hand are usually very specific and can become incredibly important to children so that those who consistently break the rules may find themselves excluded from future play by their peers.

Research indicates that some childhood games are culturally specific while others can be found in various forms across different cultures, suggesting that they perform universal functions in the natural development of children's emotional, physical and cognitive skills. Interestingly, a study carried out by Roberts and Sutton-Smith in 1962 found evidence of an association between the type of games played (whether they were predominantly based on strategy, skill or luck) and the type of upbringing of different groups of children (where the emphasis was placed on responsibility, achievement or obedience).

Of course, there is no single method or game that can be guaranteed to work for all children or to consistently help to solve particular problems or ensure certain responses. However, as facilitators, we can make a number of hypotheses about the way that children respond to play in the form of structured games. First, the way a child acts and reacts in a game situation is likely to reflect her life experiences in some way and therefore also reflect how she behaves in other situations.

So, without being overly analytical or too literal in our interpretations of children's behaviour during play, it is nevertheless important for us to be aware of general patterns. Are there children who take a long time to warm up to each game? Are there some who are 'taking over'? What happens when children become frustrated or cannot tolerate waiting their turn? Are they able to recognize personal achievements and those of others? Do they behave independently or always look to others to take the lead? Are they able to take on different roles at different times or for different types of game?

A second hypothesis that we might make centres on children's capacity for change. Working within a humanistic framework, we can approach the playing of games with the assumption that all children, whatever their current abilities, have within them the resources, and therefore the potential, for change and growth. However small or large the changes might be, the ability to respond with a degree of flexibility in different situations and the ability to learn from active participation is part of what it is to be human. Finally, we should also remember that each child's attitude to different games, his degree of participation and his enjoyment of the game will change over time as he matures and learns.

Learning opportunities

I like David Cohen's exclamation 'Ponder the irony! Children are the experts at play, play is their work and yet we, long-out-of-practice oldies, think we can teach them how to play!' (Cohen 1993, p.13) and Vivian Paley's expansion on this: 'We were taught to say that play is the work of children. But watching and listening to them, I saw that play was nothing less than Truth and Life' (Paley 1991, p.17).

Such observations once again intensify my belief that structured games played as part of an integrated approach to learning and to building self-esteem should always be used with integrity and mindfulness on the part of the facilitator. Children reinforce and experiment with a huge range of life skills (not just those that you may be hoping to target!) from repeatedly playing a variety of games – they are a powerful learning experience. However, they should not be seen as providing a measure of a child's ability. In the context of this book, they can be viewed as providing *steps* towards building and maintaining the foundation elements of self-esteem; steps that need to be continually repeated and reinforced in order to have maximum effect.

As with other self-esteem activities, games not only provide a means to address issues that have already been identified as causing some difficulties but can also be played in a pro-active way to prevent future problems from occurring. Figure 3.1 (overleaf) gives an indication of just some of the many specific and more general learning opportunities available to children through structured games sessions.

Undoubtedly, there are many more aspects that could be added according to the orientation of the group (class, occupational therapy group, speech and language therapy group, after-school group, etc.). The following chapter explores issues specifically related to working with groups and in particular to the responsibility of the facilitator in regard to structuring the emotional environment.

Specific learning/consolidation of skills

Developing spoken language skills

Developing listening skills

Developing observation skills

Ability to follow complex instructions

Ability to be reflective

Developing memory skills

Ability to give instructions

Creating new rules and conventions

Ability to take turns and tolerate waiting

Developing problem-solving skills

Ability to cooperate with group members

Building the ability to persist with an activity

Making mistakes in a safe environment

Ability to acknowledge others' actions and give feedback

Development of body image and body awareness

Understanding the different functions of games

Understanding and exploring different types of games

Using communication skills appropriately for context

Developing ability to select and modify games and rules appropriately

Learning through 'doing' not 'producing'

Exploring social and cultural aspects of games

Learning how games can reinforce previous learning

Recognizing that learning can span several subjects at once

Promoting the idea that learning is fun

Understanding rules that are made by someone else

Understanding how rules are made

Personal/social learning ———————————————————— Process learning

Building self-respect and respect of others

Understanding concepts of tolerance, fairness and empathy

Understanding concept of responsibility for own actions and how behaviour affects others

Recognizing and understanding emotions

Tolerating frustration and building emotional resilience

Reducing impulsivity and building persistence

Exploring links between thoughts, actions and feelings

Developing sensitivity to other people's strengths and difficulties

Building confidence

Building self-efficacy

Extending conscious awareness

Exploring self-concept

Building trust

Learning about the *social* value of individual achievements

Learning to be flexible in thought and action

Thinking independently and imaginatively

Learning transferable skills

Changes in attitudes or beliefs as result of learning from the social context of games

Reaching an understanding of complex experiences through a non-threatening medium

Devising own games as a result of understanding the general rules about the structure and content of games

Non-specific learning/consolidation of skills

Figure 3.1 Learning opportunities available to children through structured games

4

Working with groups

This book is by no means intended to be a groupwork manual but, in order to facilitate self-esteem games effectively, there are a few key points which I have found useful to bear in mind.

The effect of groups on individual performance

Various studies have shown that being in a group can influence behaviour in two distinct ways. Performance in a task may be improved when others are also taking part or even when they are just watching (social facilitation), but the presence of others can also result in *poorer* performance (social inhibition).

To try and account for this inconsistency, social theorist Zajonc proposed what he termed 'drive theory'. He argued that, because generally people are unpredictable (we never quite know what someone else will do), it is natural for us to be in a state of alertness when others are present. This state causes us to energize or activate our most dominant response (the one that has been learned or is most habitual). Zajonc suggested that if the task is subjectively viewed as easy then this energizing or motivating force will help us to improve our performance, but if we view the task as difficult then it will inhibit or impair our performance (Zajonc 1965).

Drive theory would predict that when children are having difficulty with a skill for which they already carry negative evaluations they will make even more mistakes when they have an audience than when they are practising alone. In contrast, if they evaluate themselves as being adept at something, their performance will be further *improved* when they have an audience. Cottrell (1972) elaborated on this theory and suggested that social presence alone is not enough to make a difference in performance levels and that *evaluation apprehension* is of greater significance. It is our concerns about how other people will evaluate us that affects our performance.

An alternative explanation to drive theory is based on self-awareness theory. This suggests that we evaluate ourselves in terms of the difference between our actual or perceived self (our self-concept) and our 'ideal' self. As we have already seen, this difference in effect gives an indication of our level of self-esteem at any given time. If the difference is large and the task is too difficult then the discrepancy between the perceived self and the ideal self can lead to us giving up. But if the difference is small and the task is perceived as relatively easy then we are more likely to be motivated to bring the two aspects of self into line. Self-awareness can, of course, be increased by the presence of others.

So how can we use this information when playing games in groups? Simple, non--competitive games are a fun way of encouraging realistic self-awareness without the added pressure of peer evaluation. Self-evaluation can take place in a safe atmosphere and has the potential to encourage increased motivation and performance rather than hinder it. The games need to be challenging but not overly difficult, capitalizing on existing skills and teaching and reinforcing new skills and insights. We also need to make sure that group members (this includes family groups) are supportive of each other's participation – even games that purport to be non-competitive can sometimes be played in a competitive way and can undermine the self-esteem of vulnerable children. This calls for conscious thought to be applied to the emotional environment in which games are played.

Structuring the emotional environment

Family therapist Virginia Satir wrote: 'Feelings of worth can only flourish in an atmosphere where individual differences are appreciated, mistakes are tolerated, communication is open, and rules are flexible – the kind of atmosphere that is found in a nurturing family' (Satir 1972, p.26). In order to facilitate this nurturing atmosphere, the three core conditions for supportive relationships proposed by Carl Rogers are useful concepts to keep in mind. These core conditions are empathy, unconditional positive regard and congruency.

Empathy

Empathy is a term freely used but often misunderstood. Rogers' own definition highlights the profound and powerful nature of an empathic relationship:

> It means entering the private perceptual world of the other and becoming thoroughly at home in it. It involves being sensitive, moment by moment, to the changing felt meanings which flow in this other person, to the fear or rage or tenderness or confusion or whatever that he or she is experiencing. It means temporarily living the other's life, moving about in it delicately without making judgements; it means sensing meanings of which he or she is scarcely aware, but not trying to uncover totally unconscious feelings since this would be too threatening… It means frequently checking with the person as to the accuracy of your sensing, and being guided by the responses you receive. (Rogers 1980, quoted in Hargarden and Sills 2002, p.35)

Unconditional positive regard

Unconditional positive regard refers to the helper's attitude towards the other person. It is an attitude of valuing the other person for who they are – an 'outgoing positive feeling without reservations, without evaluations' (Rogers 1961, p.62).

Congruency

Congruency refers to the way in which the helper is aware of his own feelings and attitudes and remains true to them. Rogers suggested that congruency engenders a sense of trust in the other person because they feel that they are with someone who is genuine.

In practical terms facilitators can demonstrate these core conditions in a number of ways. The following areas should all be given careful consideration:

- roles, rules and boundaries
- understanding and valuing emotions
- praising
- reflective practice.

Let's take each of these in turn and explore them in relation to playing games in groups.

Roles, rules and boundaries

For some children, new games can be scary and we need to spend time building trust amongst group members and between ourselves and the children we are supporting. Trust is most easily established if roles, rules and boundaries are clearly outlined at the start of a group. This can help children to feel 'contained' and safe. An example of a clear time boundary might be 'Today the games session will be ten minutes long and when we have finished the game we will do X', or 'Every morning we will play one game during circle time and then we will…'

It is also the facilitator's task to set the tone of the games and to demonstrate a firm but fair approach to prevent difficulties arising, for example from children being consistently very dominant or ridiculed by others because they do not understand the game rules. Again, this will enable the children to feel safe within the structure of the games and allow them the opportunity to experiment and explore, to expand their self-concept and to self-evaluate without fear of being judged harshly.

Because of the multi-faceted nature of games there will be multiple roles for those who choose to coordinate games sessions with young children. It is important to decide which roles you are taking on. Although these may change and evolve over time, deciding on your role and the purpose of the games you choose will help you to structure and reflect on the sessions more effectively. Possible roles might include one or more of the following:

- teacher/provider of challenges
- facilitator/encourager/enabler
- supporter/helper
- mediator/arbitrator
- observer
- participant
- researcher/information gatherer/assessor

- supervisor
- provider of fun
- ideas person.

Consider whether or not the roles you are taking on conflict in any way and, if so, on which one you need to concentrate. Perhaps a second person is needed to take a different perspective or role? For example, can you be facilitator/encourager and also record information about how individuals are coping with different aspects of a particular game?

In which role are you happiest? Do you feel most comfortable as 'provider of fun' or most comfortable in the 'teaching' role?

What about the roles of the children? These, too, may change and evolve over time so that group members each have the opportunity to be the game coordinator or the 'ideas' person or 'teacher'. Children who understand the rules of games and can explain these to others may naturally take on the role of arbitrator or game coordinator, leading others in making choices and in ensuring that the rules are understood and followed by all participants. This is a valuable skill which can be facilitated during many of the games suggested in this book. Monitoring of games by the participants themselves is an important aspect of play. Children who would normally find this role difficult can be gradually encouraged and supported in leading and monitoring fairly. Those children who have plenty of experience in arbitrating and leading games can also be encouraged to support this process by stepping back to allow others to have a go.

Games sessions also need 'rules' or guidelines to help foster the feeling of trust and safety amongst those taking part. Two of the most important rules for facilitators to make clear are:

- Children will always be given the choice of staying in or out of the game.
- Children who are reluctant to take part straight away may choose to join in at any time by giving a signal.

Understanding and valuing emotions

Young children see feelings as having certain values. They are OK or not OK; there are 'good' feelings and 'bad' feelings. Many older children continue to evaluate emotions in this way, perhaps because they don't often hear adults stating how they feel or because they're often told *not* to feel certain things – 'don't be angry', 'don't get upset' and so on. In consequence of this denial many children either 'bottle up' their feelings or stop trusting themselves and their own emotions. The message is 'don't listen to what you feel'.

If children are unaware of what they feel then eventually it will be expressed in other ways and this will affect their contact with others. For example, an initial feeling after a difficult encounter might be 'I feel bad' but this might be expressed as anger. Or they may confuse justifiable anger with feeling hurt (denying the anger).

How do we help children to be constructively aware of their emotions? The key is to acknowledge and validate feelings. For example, if a child says 'I hate this game, it's childish', think about the feeling behind the comment. Avoid interpretations but comment on what you see, hear and feel. Aim to support rather than rescue. Responses such as 'But everyone else is enjoying it, I'm sure you will too', 'You haven't tried it yet, let's have a go together' or 'That's OK, you can sit this one out if you like' would probably all get a negative reaction. But making a hypothesis about the feeling behind the words and making an appropriate comment ('It's a very noisy game and I noticed that it's hard to hear the instructions sometimes. I wonder if it would be more fun for you to stand nearer the teacher') can help the child to feel understood and is more likely to lead to him making adjustments in his self-evaluation.

Children's comments about a game may also point you in the direction of another game to address that particular issue.

Praising

Here, rather surprisingly perhaps, is a hot potato that needs careful handling! Praise is of little value if it is not genuine or has no personal meaning for the child. If praise does not resonate with his self-concept and self-evaluations he is very likely to reject it. Also, unrealistic or unjustified praise could set him up for experiencing lower self-esteem if he tries to do things before he is ready or if it leads to him developing unrealistically high expectations of what he can achieve. Unfortunately, even when adults do offer genuine praise this can so frequently be followed by a qualification of some sort, negating the praise completely. Such qualified praise might go something like:

> 'What a lovely picture – but you've forgotten his eyes!'
>
> 'Well done for tidying up – why can't you always do that?'
>
> 'There, I knew you'd get that sum right – you just haven't been concentrating.'

The most effective approach is to use genuine specific, descriptive praise whenever possible.

Adele Faber and Elaine Mazlish, authors of *How to Talk So Kids Will Listen and Listen So Kids Will Talk*, point out that helpful praise comes in two parts: '1. The adult describes with appreciation what he or she sees or feels. 2. The child, after hearing the description, is then able to praise himself' (Faber and Mazlish 1982, p.176). One of the authors gives an example from her experience with her own child of four who showed her a page of 'scribble' that he had brought home from nursery school and asked, 'Is it good?' This is how she reports the conversation:

> 'Well, I see you went circle, circle, circle...wiggle, wiggle, wiggle...dot, dot, dot, dot, dot, dot, dot, and slash, slash!'
>
> 'Yeah!' he nodded enthusiastically.
>
> I said, 'How did you ever think to do this?'
>
> He thought awhile. 'Because I'm an artist,' he said.
>
> I thought, 'It's a remarkable process. The adult describes, and the child really does praise himself.'

> (Faber and Mazlish 1982, p.176)

So, for example, instead of saying 'you're very good at playing this game' or 'you're brilliant at drawing' you might describe what the child has done: 'You listened really carefully in that game so you knew exactly how to guess the code. Well done!'

Use memory aids if necessary to remember what children have done in previous games sessions. Non-judgemental comments on past experiences and actions can be extremely motivating and self-affirming for children.

Reflective practice

Most groups benefit from having at least two facilitators. It is very difficult to 'hold' a group and to be aware of everything that is going on within and between all the group members if you are working on your own. Having two facilitators gives you the chance to share ideas, keep better track of what is happening and obviously share the responsibility for planning, carrying out and evaluating the sessions. It is also important for each facilitator to be able to reflect on his or her skills as a group leader and to be able to debrief at the end of each session. This is much harder if you are only able to do this infrequently with a peer or at a scheduled supervision session.

I know from experience how exhausting it can be to facilitate a group and keep an eye on what is going on for all the children, and I can only guess at how challenging and time-consuming it must be for teachers to be constantly monitoring and setting targets for individuals in a large class.

When I was regularly running intensive courses for young children who stammer I would sit with my colleagues at the end of each day and discuss each child in turn (usually between 12 and 15 children). We would make notes on aspects such as observable behaviour and reported feelings, interaction skills, speech and language skills, general demeanour, ability to problem-solve and so on. In addition we would add perspectives from parents gathered during parent meetings run in parallel to the children's group. We would then set targets for the next day. We always seemed to take longer than we had planned for this task and all too often there was little or no time for reflecting on the whole process of the day and giving feedback to each other.

Yet when we *did* take time to do this, we found ourselves much more able to deal with the challenges and joys of the next day and to monitor our own facilitation skills in ways that were most likely to support the children. An added aspect, of course, was that team discussions and realistic self-evaluations helped to strengthen both our personal and our team esteem.

The importance of reflective practice lies in the way that we use it to develop the most effective way of working. In this context we obviously need to be aware of our own feelings and needs and the way in which what we do and say has a direct effect on the children in our care. Most professions now have their own guidelines for reflective practice. The following suggestions are offered as a supplement to existing frameworks and as a focus for anyone who is not used to working in this way.

Before you embark on a new games session there are a few questions which you might want to ask yourself.

- What is my role as the game coordinator?
- Why are we playing these particular games? What are my aims/intended outcomes?
- How will I know if I've achieved my aims/outcomes?
- What are my personal feelings about these games?
- Are the games appropriate for the age/cultural background/sex of the children in the group?
- Do I know the 'rules' of the games?
- What do I think will work well in this session?
- Who (if anyone) in the group will find the games difficult/challenging/easy?
- Do I need to adapt the games in any way to allow/encourage full participation of all group members?
- What back-up strategies will I need?
- How will I handle behaviour that is potentially disruptive to the group?
- Am I aware of why this behaviour might occur?
- If the group is large or diverse in needs do I have a 'support' person available?
- What will I do if a child knows a different version of a game and wants to play that? (For example, you might suggest that you play their version next time or it might be appropriate to share different versions at the time and abandon one of the other games you had planned.)
- Is this the right time for the game(s)?
- Is the room the right temperature?
- Am I feeling up to it?

After completion of a games session take a few moments as soon as you can to reflect on the game(s) you chose to play. What went well? Was there anything that was difficult to monitor? What skills did you use? You might find it helpful to use the questions listed above to guide you in this reflective process and to help you to make any adjustments necessary in preparation for the next session.

Make notes against the relevant games and try to make time to discuss your ideas and reflections with at least one other person. Remember, reflective practice is not about being judgemental about our own abilities. It is about reflecting on our skills and on our learning and on our ways of navigating any difficulties.

So, the theory finished with, let's get going and *play some games!*

Bibliography

Antidote (2003) *The Emotional Literacy Handbook: Promoting Whole-School Strategies.* London: David Fulton Publishers.

Brandes, D. and Phillips, H. (1979) *Gamesters' Handbook: 140 Games for Teachers and Group Leaders.* London: Hutchinson.

Bruner, J.S., Jolly, A. and Sylva, K. (eds) (1976) *Play: Its Role in Development and Evolution.* Harmondsworth: Penguin.

Ellis, M.J. (1973) *Why People Play.* Englewood Cliffs, NJ: Prentice Hall.

Hogg, M.A. and Vaughan, M. (2002) *Social Psychology* (3rd edition). Harlow: Prentice Hall.

Madders, J. (1987) *Relax and be Happy.* London: Unwin Paperbacks.

Masheder, M. (1989) *Let's Play Together.* London: Green Print.

Neelands, J. (1990) *Structuring Drama Work: A Handbook of Available Forms in Theatre and Drama.* Cambridge: Cambridge University Press.

Payne, H. (1990) *Creative Movement and Dance in Groupwork.* Bicester: Winslow Press.

Plummer, D. (2006) *The Adventures of the Little Tin Tortoise: A Self-Esteem Story with Activities for Teachers, Parents and Carers.* London: Jessica Kingsley Publishers.

Robinson, J.P., Shaver, P.R. and Wrightsman, L.S. (eds) (1991) *Measures of Personality and Social Psychological Attitudes.* Vol. 1 in *Measures of Social Psychological Attitude Series.* London and San Diego: Academic Press.

Sher, B. (1998) *Self-esteem Games. 300 Fun Activities that Make Children Feel Good about Themselves.* New York: John Wiley & Sons, Inc.

References

Bandura, A. (1977) 'Self-efficacy: Toward a unifying theory of behaviour change.' *Psychological Review 84*, 191–215.

Burns, R.B. (1979) *The Self Concept in Theory, Measurement, Development and Behaviour.* New York: Longman.

Butler, R.J. (2001) *The Self Image Profiles.* London: The Psychological Corporation.

Butler, R.J. and Gasson, S.L. (2005) 'Self esteem/self concept scales for children and adolescents: A review.' *Child and Adolescent Mental Health 10*, 4, 190–201.

California Task Force to Promote Self-Esteem and Personal and Social Responsibility (1990) *Toward a State of Self-Esteem.* Sacramento: California State Department of Education.

Cohen, D. (1993) *The Development of Play* (2nd edition). London: Routledge.

Coopersmith, S. (1967) *The Antecedents of Self-Esteem.* San Francisco: W.H. Freeman and Company.

Cottrell, N.B. (1972) 'Social Facilitation.' In C. McClintock (ed.) *Experimental Social Psychology.* New York: Holt, Rinehart & Winston.

Eliot, L. (1999) *What's Going on in There? How the Brain and Mind Develop in the First Five Years of Life.* London: Bantam.

Faber, A. and Mazlish, E. (1982) *How to Talk So Kids Will Listen and Listen So Kids Will Talk.* New York: Avon.

Garvey, C. (1977) *Play.* London: Fontana/Open Books.

Glouberman, D. (2003) *Life Choices, Life Changes: Develop your Personal Vision with Imagework.* London: Hodder and Stoughton.

Gurney, P. (1988) *Self-Esteem in Children with Special Educational Needs.* London and New York: Routledge.

Hargarden, H. and Sills, C. (2002) *Transactional Analysis: A Relational Perspective.* Hove and New York: Brunner-Routledge.

Harter, S. (1999) *The Construction of the Self.* New York: Guilford Press.

Hillman, J. (2002) *Healing Fiction.* Putnam, Connecticut: Spring Publications, Inc.

Johnson, R.A. (1989) *Inner Work: Using Dreams and Active Imagination for Personal Growth.* New York: HarperSanFrancisco.

Mruk, C.J. (1999) *Self-Esteem: Research, Theory and Practice* (2nd edition). London: Free Association Books.

Opie, I. and Opie, P. (1976) 'Street Games: Counting-out and Chasing.' In J.S. Bruner, A. Jolly and K. Sylva (eds) *Play: Its Role in Development and Evolution.* Harmondsworth: Penguin.

Paley, V.G. (1991) *The Boy Who Would Be a Helicopter.* London: Harvard University Press.

Plummer, D. (1999) *Using Interactive Imagework with Children: Walking on the Magic Mountain.* London: Jessica Kingsley Publishers.

Plummer, D. (2001) *Helping Children to Build Self-Esteem.* London: Jessica Kingsley Publishers.

Plummer, D. (2005) *Helping Adolescents and Adults to Build Self-Esteem.* London: Jessica Kingsley Publishers.

Roberts, J.M. and Sutton-Smith, B. (1962) 'Child training and game involvement.' *Ethnology 1,* 166–185.

Rogers, C.R. (1961) *On Becoming a Person: A Therapist's View of Psychotherapy.* London: Constable.

Rogers, C.R. (1980) *A Way of Being.* Boston: Houghton Mifflin.

Rogers, C.R. and Dymond, R.F. (eds) (1954) *Psychotherapy and Personality Change: Coordinated Studies in the Client-centred Approach.* Chicago: University of Chicago Press.

Rosenberg, M.J. (1965) *Society and Adolescent Self-image.* Princeton, NJ: Princeton University Press.

Rosenberg, M. and Simmons, R.G. (1972) *Black and White Self-Esteem: The Urban School Child.* Washington, DC: American Sociological Association.

Satir, V. (1972) *Peoplemaking.* London: Souvenir Press.

Zajonc, R.B. (1965) 'Social facilitation.' *Science 149,* 269–274.

Part Two

Games for self-esteem

For ease of reference, the games have been marked with a set of symbols to indicate age-appropriateness and the amount of speaking involved. The symbols used are as follows:

⑤	This gives an indication of the suggested *youngest* age for playing the game. There is no upper age limit.
⏲ 10 mins	An approximate time is given for the length of the game (excluding the discussion time). This will obviously vary according to the size of group and the ability of the players.
♦ ♦ ♦	Indicates that the game is suitable for larger groups (eight or more).
♦ ♦	The game is suitable for small groups.
♡♡♡	The game involves a lot of speaking unless it is adapted.
♡♡	A moderate amount of speaking is required by players.
♡	The game is primarily a non-verbal game or one requiring minimal speech.
☑ observation	This gives an indication of an additional key skill used or developed by playing this game.

5

Non-competitive ways to choose groups and leaders

It is worth having several different methods of dividing children into groups or pairs or choosing someone to lead a game. For the purpose of these games we want to avoid placing children in a position where they are anxiously waiting to be 'picked' or where the same groups or pairs consistently choose to work together. The following methods are just some of the many ways in which to encourage random selections.

To choose a leader

- Have names in a hat or in separate balloons. Children pick a name or pop a balloon to see who is the leader for that session. This ensures that everyone gets a turn eventually.

- Take turns according to dates of birth (e.g. using just the date in the month).

To choose pairs

- Count round half the circle then start again. The 'one's work together, 'two's work together, etc.
- Put two sets of matching objects in a 'lucky dip' box. Children draw out an object and find their partner who has a matching object.
- Stand in a circle eyes closed and arms outstretched. Walk across the circle until you meet someone else.

To choose groups

- Sit in a large circle. Count round in sets of two or four or however many small groups are needed. 'One's then work together, 'two's work together, etc.
- Count round the circle using colour names, with as many different colours as are needed for the number of groups.
- Deal out playing cards, e.g. all the clubs in one group and diamonds in the other.

6

Warm-ups and ice-breakers

These are an essential part of group sessions, particularly if you are starting a new group, intending to play several games in one session, or a new member is joining an existing group.

Warm-ups and ice-breakers help children to feel comfortable in a group, encourage them to interact with each other, and help them to feel that they have been acknowledged by everyone else. They act as a ritual to mark the beginning of a session and to ensure that each person has fully 'arrived' in the group. They also foster group cohesion and help to develop a group identity.

What's my name?

⑦
🕐 10 mins
👤 👤 👤
💬💬💬

☑ taking turns
☑ concentration
☑ observation

☑ listening
☑ asking questions
☑ memory

A fun way to encourage children to interact at the start of a new group.

How to play

Players write their name (or how they would like to be known) on a sticky label. They hide the label somewhere on their own clothes, for example in the top of their sock, in a pocket, under their collar or on the sole of their shoe.

Children try to find as many names as possible (within a time limit suitable for the size of the group) without touching anyone. They can only ask questions such as 'Is it on the sole of your shoe?' or 'Can you show me underneath your right foot?' They either write down all the names that they find or try to remember them.

When the time limit is up everyone stands or sits in a circle. The game coordinator stands behind each person in turn and everyone tries to remember that person's name.

Adaptations
⑤
💬

Throw a soft cushion around the group. Each child says her own name when she catches it. After everyone has had a turn, go round again. This time the rest of the group say the name of the child who catches the cushion.

Put name labels in a bowl. Each child picks out another child's name and tries to find that person in the group and present them with the label.

Make two sets of animal picture labels: one for children to wear and one to put in the bowl. Children pick an animal label from the bowl and find the matching picture worn by a group member.

Reflection

What helps you to remember other people's names? What does it feel like when other people remember your name?

Notes

Guess the voice

⑤
🕐 10 mins
👤 👤 👤
💬

☑ listening
☑ deduction
☑ memory

☑ taking turns
☑ concentration

How to play   Players stand or sit in a circle. Each player invents a unique vocal call, for example a combination of vowels with different intonation patterns or a hum or a whistle. The whole group listens to each call in turn as the players say their first name and then their chosen sound.

One person stands in the centre of the circle with a blindfold on. The game coordinator silently chooses someone to make their call. The person in the centre tries to name the caller. If they get it right they can have a second turn.

Each person has a maximum of two turns before the coordinator chooses another person to be in the centre.

Adaptations   Two or more people call at the same time.

Two people stand in the centre and can confer about the name of the caller.

The person who was last in the centre can choose the next caller.

Everyone changes seats before the caller is chosen.

The players are split into pairs to practise their calls. One child from each pair then stands in the centre of the circle and is blindfolded. On a signal their partners make their chosen calls. The players who are blindfolded have to carefully move around the circle until they find their partner.

Reflection   How do we recognize individual voices? What makes our voices different? What might happen if we all sounded exactly the same? What words can we use to describe different voices (e.g. deep, gruff, loud, soft, like chocolate)? Keep these descriptions very general, rather than specific to individual children.

Notes

Signs and signatures

⑦
🕐 5 mins
👤 👤 👤
💬💬

☑ listening
☑ memory
☑ taking turns

☑ concentration
☑ observation
☑ non-verbal
   communication

How to play
Sit in a circle. The first player says their name accompanied by a movement/gesture (e.g. head movement, clapping, making sweeping gesture with both hands). The next child introduces the previous child (using their name and gesture) and then says their own name accompanied by their own gesture.

This is _____ and I am _____.

Finish with everyone saying and gesturing their own name at the same time.

Adaptations
⑤
💬

Players say their own name and think of a gesture but do not need to introduce anyone. Use gesture/movement without saying names.

Play the game standing up and include large movements such as jump back, shake leg, hop.

Teach the children specific signs, such as finger spelling for their initials or signs for different animals.

In smaller groups players can try and remember the names and gestures of as many previous players as possible (in a similar way to a game of 'I went shopping and I bought…').

Reflection
If you had a different name, would you choose a different gesture?

Experiment with several famous names and see if the group can come to an agreement about the appropriate type of movement to associate with each name.

Notes

Name fame

⑦
🕐 5 mins
🧍 🧍
💬

☑ listening
☑ taking turns
☑ concentration

☑ observation
☑ imagination
☑ dramatic awareness

How to play   Players stand or sit in a circle. The game coordinator demonstrates a style of speech such as in the style of an adoring pop fan, a queen or king, a magician, a musical conductor or a famous hero/heroine. 'Overplay' the styles as much as possible! The children say their own names around the circle in this style. Repeat this with several different styles. Each player in turn then tells the group how they would like to hear their name. Everyone repeats the person's name in the chosen style at the same time.

Adaptations   Try varying different speech parameters, e.g. saying names very quietly, loudly, slowly, quickly, with a high pitch, low pitch or different combinations of these.

Say names with different emotional emphases, e.g. grumpily, happily, sadly, courageously.

Reflection   Our names are a very important part of who we are. How do we hear our names used? Lovingly, angrily, accusingly, melodiously?! How would we like to hear them used in this group? Can you always tell what someone is feeling when they say your name? How can you tell? Are you always right?

Notes

Fruit salad

⑤
🕐 5 mins
👤 👤 👤
💬

☑ listening
☑ memory
☑ categorization

☑ concentration
☑ observation

This is a fast-paced game that can easily be adapted to suit different likes and dislikes. For that reason it can be played many times in different formats and is always a favourite amongst groups of active children!

How to play Sit in a circle with one person standing in the centre. Each person chooses the name of a different fruit. The person in the centre calls out two fruits. These two children swap places and the caller tries to sit in one of their seats before the other person gets there. If the caller says 'fruit salad' everyone swaps seats! The person left standing is the next caller.

Adaptations Motorway – using car names

Zoo-keeper – using animal names

School dinners – selection of different meals

Pop stars

and anything else that comes in groups!

For larger groups and the younger age range have a limited number of items so that there is more than one child for each one (four apples, four bananas, etc.). This can get quite hectic with lots of children running across the circle at the same time, so take care!

Reflection Do different children like different versions? Why?

What might be some different reasons for liking/disliking different types of games? (See the Appendix for examples of different types of games.)

What is your favourite outdoor game? What is your favourite indoor game?

What do all games have in common?

Notes

Silent greetings

⑤   ☑ memory   ☑ observation
🕐 10 mins   ☑ taking turns   ☑ non-verbal
👤 👤 👤   ☑ concentration   communication
💬

This game requires plenty of space for the children to move around freely.

How to play Everyone walks slowly around the room, silently greeting each other in a friendly way. For example, a little wave, a long slow wave, offering 'high five', smiling, making eye-contact, having a short 'conversation' between hands. The game coordinator may need to demonstrate a few ideas first. There should be no physical contact during this. The aim is to see how many different ways players can greet each other successfully.

Adaptation Play a variety of music (e.g. culturally specific music, lively music, slow, gentle music) while the children walk around the room and greet each other in ways that match the different rhythms and themes.

Reflection Did you learn a new greeting or get a new idea and then try it out on someone else? Did some ways of greeting seem easier than others? What was the most fun/natural/relaxed way to greet others? Which one felt most like 'you'? Did you change your greetings to match other people or did pairs sometimes greet each other in completely different ways? How did that feel?

Notes

Run-around

⑤

🕐 5 mins

👤 👤

💬

☑ taking turns   ☑ self-awareness
☑ cooperation   ☑ concentration

How to play   One child is chosen to start the game off (child A). The rest of the players stand in a close circle, facing the centre. Child A walks slowly around the outside of the circle and taps someone on the shoulder. That person and child A then run in opposite directions around the outside of the circle to see who can get back to the space first. The player left out of the circle then walks slowly around the outside and chooses another person by tapping them on the shoulder.

Adaptation   Players hop in opposite directions to get to the available space.

Reflection   What do you do when you want to join a group who are already playing or working together? What could you say to the group? When is it easy to join a group? When might it be difficult?

Notes

Magic threes

⑦

🕒 10 mins

☑ trust
☑ listening
☑ memory

☑ taking turns
☑ concentration

How to play

Players have three minutes to walk around the room and introduce themselves to three other people. Each child tells these three people three important facts about themselves. For younger children this could be full name, something I hate and something I like. For older children this could be my greatest achievement, my best birthday and my most treasured possession.

When the time is up, everyone sits in a circle and recounts as much information about as many other children as possible.

Adaptation

Pairs share the information and then introduce each other to the rest of the group.

Reflection

How difficult or easy was it to remember what you heard? What would make it easier/harder to remember facts about other people? Why is it important to remember what people tell us about themselves? What does it feel like when someone remembers something important about you? What does it feel like when people get the facts wrong?

Notes

Our story

⑤
🕐 5 mins
👤 👤
💬

☑ self-control   ☑ listening
☑ self-awareness ☑ concentration

This is a variation of a popular game called 'The old family coach'.

How to play — The game coordinator makes up a short story about the group, using each child's name at least three times. When the child hears their own name they stand up, turn round three times and take a bow! When they hear '*all the children*' or '*everyone*' they all stand up, turn round three times and take a bow.

For example: 'The new classroom was ready at last and *all the children* waited excitedly in the playground on the first day of term. The head teacher asked *Edward* and *Jodie* to fetch the registers from the office. On the way inside they bumped into *Karen* and *Amarjeet* who had gone to fetch the school bell. *Sam* was allowed to ring the bell and he rang it so loudly that *Marcus* and *Sandeep* put their hands over their ears. Then *Edward* and *Michèle* led *everyone* into their new classroom…' and so on.

Adaptations — Use a response that requires only slight or no physical movement.

Use musical instruments for children to signal when they hear their name.

Tell a story about going to the zoo. The children choose an animal and make the appropriate animal noise when they hear their name.

Reflection — Saying someone's name is a good way to get their attention. What else is it OK to do when we want to say something to someone who doesn't seem to be listening? What is it not OK to do?

Notes

The rule of the realm

⑦
🕐 10 mins
👤 👤 👤
💬💬💬

- ☑ listening
- ☑ cooperation
- ☑ memory

- ☑ deduction
- ☑ problem-solving
- ☑ observation

This game encourages players to work together in order to solve a puzzle about group rules.

How to play   Divide the group into two. Group A leaves the room. Group B makes up a 'talking rule' such as 'every time you speak you must cross your arms' or 'every time you finish speaking you must scratch your head'. The game coordinator checks that everyone in group B remembers to do this by asking each one a simple question such as 'Do you like chocolate?' or 'How old are you?' Group A returns to the room and the coordinator repeats the previous questions or asks similar ones while group A observe. The aim is for group A to guess the rule. The emphasis is on group problem-solving – if one person in group A guesses the correct rule, this means that the whole group have achieved. Older children can therefore be encouraged to confer before they guess the rule.

Adaptations   Allow a maximum of five guesses.

Rules for older and very able children can be quite complex such as 'when the coordinator asks you a question it is the person on your left who answers' or 'you have to use the last word from the question to start your answer'.

All the group stay in the room and the coordinator chooses a place to set up his or her kingdom, e.g. 'the moon', 'the playground'. Each person says what they will bring if they are chosen to be part of the new kingdom. The rule that they have to discover either relates to the first letter of their own name or relates to the first letter of the place where the kingdom will be. The coordinator starts by giving a few examples such as '*S*andip would be welcome in the new kingdom if he brought *s*nakes with him but not if he brought *m*oney. *M*iriam would be welcome if she brought *m*oney, but definitely not if she brought *j*ewels.' The coordinator tells group members if they can join the kingdom or not according to what they offer to bring with them. This needs a strict time limit and therefore clues may need to be made more and more obvious to give everyone the chance to guess the 'rule' and join the kingdom! Children should be encouraged to help each other out towards the end of the game in order to ensure that no one is left out!

Reflection   Do all groups need rules? Why/why not? Are some rules more useful than others?

What does it feel like to not know a group rule when it seems like everyone else knows it? What should groups do about that?

Notes

Additional notes: more ideas for warm-ups and ice-breakers

Reflections

Who am I?

Foundation element: self-knowledge

Children love to hear and to tell stories about themselves. Familiar themes might be 'Tell me the story about when I was born' or 'What happened when I had to go to hospital when I was a baby?' or 'Do you remember when I got that prize/got bullied/fell over/climbed the tree…?' Even when parents have related the same story on several different occasions there is often still a need to hear it many more times! This is a major way in which we learn about ourselves – by repeatedly hearing and telling our stories.

A strong sense of 'self' and a sense of 'belonging' are vital elements of healthy self-esteem. It is important for children to know something about their history and to discover more about who they are and how they fit in to the family and the wider groups to which they belong.

The games in this section encourage self-exploration on many different levels including exploration of how we are different from others in looks and character, how we can also have things in common with others and the importance of valuing both diversity and similarity.

Figure me out!

⑨

🕐 **60 mins**

♀ ♀ ♀

♡

☑ self-awareness   ☑ observation
☑ creative thinking ☑ understanding
☑ concentration   metaphors

This requires some preparation by the game coordinator beforehand.

How to play
Divide the group into two halves. Groups A and B then work in different rooms or in different parts of the same room but must not look at what the other group is doing. Within each group children work in pairs or threes to draw round each other's body outline on large pieces of paper. Each child uses pictures from comics, catalogues, magazines, etc. to 'clothe' their body outline with things that represent something about who they are and what they like to do.

Group A try to guess who each of the pictures belong to in group B and vice versa.

Adaptations
⑤
Once clothed, add words, headlines and catchphrases to represent personality strengths.

Younger children can simply draw around each other's body shapes or this can be done by a helper. They then add a face and colour in the clothes.

Reflection
How did you work out which figure represented which person? Did you discover anything about another person that you hadn't known before?

When you stand back and look at all the figures can you see anything that any of them have in common? What are the main differences?

Which aspect(s) of your own picture would you most like other people to remember?

Notes

Story-line

⑦
🕐 10 mins
✓ listening
✓ memory
✓ research skills
✓ planning
✓ sequencing/story-telling

The children will need to do some research at home before this game can be played.

How to play Set children the task of researching their names in preparation for a subsequent session. Guide them with questions such as 'Do you know what your name means? How was your name chosen? How important is your name to you? When you use your name, how do you use it? Do you like other people to use your full name or a shortened version or do you have a favourite nickname?'

In the circle start by telling name stories in pairs. Each pair then takes turns to introduce their partner to the group and say one thing they remembered about that child's name story.

Adaptations Research middle names.

In smaller groups take time to hear each child's name story in the circle.

Reflection Do you know anyone else with the same name as you? Are they anything like you or are they very different? How many children have names that are a 'family' name, given to successive generations perhaps? How do they feel about that?

Notes

If I were an animal

⑤

🕐 10 mins

🚶 🚶 🚶

🗩

☑ imagination
☑ self-awareness
☑ understanding opposites

☑ non-verbal communication
☑ understanding characteristics

This game requires a large space for the children to be able to move around.

How to play

Take some time to brainstorm animal names and characteristics.

Each child thinks of an animal that somehow shows something about who they are. Divide the group into two. Half the group imagine becoming their chosen animal for a short while – moving around the room, greeting other animals and finding out their 'character'. The other half of the group sit and watch. Their task is to guess all the animals as quickly as possible. As soon as an animal is correctly identified it must sit down. Keep going until all the animals have been guessed. The groups then swap over.

Adaptations

The game coordinator chooses one of the animals from the above game. Everyone in the group tries to act like that animal for 30 seconds. The person who originally chose the animal (in the first game) can give 'directions', e.g. 'I'm a flamingo and I move like this. I speak like this. I don't like…but I do like… When I meet other flamingos I…' There is no 'correct' way to explore being this animal – for example, it doesn't matter if the child says 'I'm a flamingo and I like to eat chocolate'!

Everyone will need a turn at directing others in how to be their animal so it is best to do this version of the game with small groups or in pairs.

Ask the children to choose a completely different animal, perhaps one who has the opposite characteristic to the first one chosen. For example, if a child chose a noisy animal they could try being a quiet one, fast/slow, big/small, etc.

All the children go back to being the original animals and stand or sit in a circle to introduce themselves to the group and say one good thing about being this animal (e.g. 'I am a leopard and I can run very fast'). Finish by 'stepping out' of the chosen animals – invite the children to have a stretch and shake their arms and legs and go back to being children again.

Reflection   What did it feel like to be the animal that you chose? How are you like that animal? Did you find out anything new about anyone else?

Do you think you are sometimes like the first animal and sometimes like the second one? How does that feel? Talk about how we can have different levels of the same feeling or characteristic in different situations – like having a volume control or an intensity control – for example, we could be energetic one minute and very sleepy the next; or happy and then suddenly sad; timid in one situation and very brave in another.

How did it feel to be like someone else (their chosen animal)? Was it easy or difficult? Are you ever like that yourself?

Notes

Living links

⑤

🕐 10 mins

�; �; �;

♡

☑ listening

☑ self-awareness

☑ taking turns

☑ concentration

☑ observation

How to play   The game coordinator chooses someone to start off a living link. This person calls to another member of the group who has something physically in common with him, e.g. both wearing glasses or both wearing black shoes. This second person holds hands with the first and then calls to a third who has something else in common with her. This continues until all players are connected.

Adaptations   Stay seated in the circle and use string to connect players instead of holding hands.

No repetitions of similarities allowed. Everyone has to think of a new 'feature' that they have in common with the next person to be called.

Groups that know each other well enough can connect according to likes/dislikes, hobbies, names, number of brothers or sisters, etc.

Everyone walks around the room trying to find someone with whom they have at least three things in common.

Reflection   Everyone has something in common with someone else.

Talk about the variety of similarities.

Notes

Emblems

⑦
🕐 45 mins
♟ ♟ ♟
◯

☑ imagination   ☑ self-respect
☑ deduction   ☑ understanding
☑ self-awareness   metaphors

How to play   Players each draw the shape of a shield on a large piece of paper. Divide the shield into four sections and draw different symbols/pictures in each section to show:

- my special talents and skills

- special people in my life

- my special place

- my proudest moment/important achievements.

Display the shields on a table or wall. Players guess the owner of each one.

Adaptations   Draw a shield for my hopes for next year; my motto.

Make one large coat of arms for the whole group.

Make a flag instead of a shield.

Reflection   Talk about similarities and differences between the shields.

Talk about and celebrate the achievements, talents and skills.

How easy or difficult was it for you to think of positive things to put on your shield?

Notes

Fingerprinting

⑤   ☑ imagination   ☑ dramatic awareness
🕐 20 mins   ☑ planning   ☑ sequencing/story-telling
👤 👤 👤   ☑ self-awareness
💬💬

How to play	Each child uses their own unique fingerprint(s) as a starting point for a drawing or painting of a person. Cut out the figure and make up a short puppet show in which the figure tells something about himself or herself to the rest of the group.
Adaptations	Draw round each other's hands and add fingerprints to each finger.
	Put individual prints onto cards and try to guess whose prints they are.
Reflection	Talk about the uniqueness of fingerprints and each of us being unique individuals.
Notes	

Tell me my story

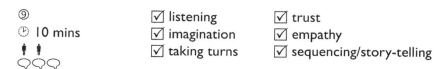

⑨
🕐 10 mins
🚶 🚶
🗨🗨🗨

☑ listening
☑ imagination
☑ taking turns

☑ trust
☑ empathy
☑ sequencing/story-telling

A wonderful game to play at home as children love to hear the story of big events in their lives – often over and over again!

How to play   The game coordinator provides a title which includes a child's name such as:

- Marcus the bold
- Amazing Craig
- Javed's dream day out
- Katie's greatest adventure.

The child in question starts off the story. The rest of the group continue around the circle, saying one sentence each. This could be a completely imaginary story or could relate to something that everyone knows really happened.

Adaptations   Have a selection of three or four titles written up so that each child can choose their own title.

Encourage the children to think up their own title for their story.

Reflection   Was this difficult, exciting, funny, easy? Did the group come up with some things that truly reflected the child's personality/likes and dislikes?

How did it feel to listen to a story about yourself?

Notes

Walk this way

⑤
🕐 10 mins
🚶 🚶 🚶
💬

☑ empathy
☑ imagination
☑ observation

☑ non-verbal
   communication
☑ dramatic awareness

How to play   The game coordinator asks a 'leader' to walk around the room in a chosen way, e.g. like a giant, like the world's strongest man, or like an older person who has stiff joints. Everyone watches closely and then tries to walk in exactly the same way. When the game coordinator rings a bell or shakes a tambourine everyone 'freezes' in one position. They hold this position for the count of five. Then someone else leads the group in a different type of walk until the coordinator rings the bell again. Continue for at least five different walks.

Adaptations   Walk in different ways to reflect different emotions.

In pairs try and exactly mirror how your partner walks across the room.

Reflection   Discuss similarities and differences in the way that people walk. Think about 'sameness' and differences in such things as looks, actions, likes and dislikes. What would the world be like if we all talked and moved in exactly the same way? Why would that be difficult? And *then* what would happen? How does it feel to 'walk in someone else's shoes'? How does it feel when someone else really tries to feel what it is like to be you?

Notes

True or false?

⑦
🕐 5 mins
👤 👤 👤
💬💬

☑ taking turns
☑ deduction
☑ trust

☑ listening
☑ imagination

How to play   Everyone walks around the room introducing themselves to each other and saying two things about themselves. One of these is true and the other is false. Partners guess which is the false statement and which is the true one.

Adaptations   In the circle, tell three amazing things about yourself, two of them false and one of them true. The group vote on which one is true.

Children introduce themselves to one other person who then introduces them to the group, telling the amazing (true) fact.

Reflection   What is the difference between boasting and being proud about something? Are there any amazing facts that you would like to celebrate with the group? What are some of the different *types* of amazing facts that people invented?

Notes

I can, you can

⑤
🕐 5 mins
👤 👤 👤
💬💬

☑ taking turns	☑ trust
☑ listening	☑ concentration
☑ observation	

How to play   Players brainstorm a list of actions that everyone could do. Children volunteer to perform one of these for the rest of the group to copy. Each child who volunteers says 'my name is…and I can… (hop, clap, stand on one leg, twirl, jump, etc.)'. The rest of the children then all take one step forward, perform the action for five seconds and then step back and wait for the next volunteer.

Adaptation   Play music while the children 'disco' dance in a circle. Volunteers take one step forward and show a dance 'move' for everyone else to copy.

Reflection   Talk about what it feels like to move freely and not worry about 'getting it right'.

What does it feel like to have others try and follow your dance?

Notes

Additional notes: more ideas for self-knowledge games

Reflections

8

Friends and feelings

Foundation element: self and others

The games in this section explore aspects of group cooperation and trust and aim to promote an understanding of how our thoughts and actions affect our relationships with other people.

Understanding relationships also involves understanding feelings. During childhood we begin to learn about our emotions and how to understand the emotions that other people may be experiencing without being swamped by them. It is important to help children to understand that all feelings are valid and that they can have some control over the ways in which they express how they feel.

By valuing their own feelings and by facing difficult or confusing situations and coping with them successfully children will be able to confidently and creatively meet new challenges and develop their skills, so further strengthening their feelings of self-worth and self-efficacy. They will also develop a healthy level of 'emotional resilience': the ability to cope with temporary feelings of helplessness, frustration or upset without being engulfed by them or experiencing them as failure.

Group drawing

⑤
🕐 30 mins
† † †
💬

☑ cooperation   ☑ imagination
☑ concentration   ☑ observation
☑ sharing

How to play   Set out large sheets of paper on tables so that groups of children can move around their table easily. Each group draws a collaborative picture or just 'makes marks' on the paper, using a variety of pencils, pastels and pens. The group coordinator can provide a theme or leave the children to draw whatever they like.

Adaptation   Draw pictures in pairs. Divide a piece of paper in two so that pairs can draw at the same time or take turns.

Reflection   How do we maintain group cooperation?

What does it feel like to draw a joint picture? How did you feel when someone drew their image very close to yours or changed your image in some way? What was the difference between all drawing different things on the same piece of paper and all drawing a truly collaborative picture?

Notes

Vocal orchestra

⑥
🕐 5 mins
👤 👤 👤
💬

☑ listening
☑ cooperation
☑ concentration

☑ observation
☑ non-verbal
   communication

How to play   The game coordinator demonstrates how to 'conduct' an orchestra with hand movements that indicate, e.g. loudly/softly, quickly/slowly, all join in, stop.

Each child chooses a vocalization (see 'Guess the voice', page 40). Players stand in a row, in small groups or in a circle according to the size of the group. Conductors take turns to conduct the orchestra as a whole group and with duos, solos, etc.

Adaptations   Use movements instead of sounds, e.g. hop, jump, stretch, wave.

⑤   Divide the group up into smaller groups of four before starting. The smaller groups stand together and all do the action or make the same sound when the conductor points to them.

Use home-made instruments.

Reflection   What does it feel like to be the conductor? What does it feel like to be part of the orchestra? What are some of the difficulties involved in being a conductor? What does it feel like to do a solo or duo when you are part of an orchestra?

Notes

Blind walk

⑧
🕐 15 mins

✓ trust
✓ cooperation
✓ listening

✓ supporting
✓ giving instructions
✓ empathy

This game requires plenty of space for players to move around in. A few large obstacles can be used for players to negotiate.

How to play   Divide the group into two. One half of the group will act as silent 'protectors' while the other half of the group is led on a blind walk. The protectors will gently prevent the 'explorers' from walking into obstacles or each other (e.g. by touching them on the arm if they get too close). The explorers choose one leader whom they trust to lead them around the room in a snake formation (with the leader as the head of the snake). Each explorer puts one hand on the shoulder of the person in front of them. The game coordinator, the protectors and the line leader all keep their eyes open. The leader can give verbal instructions. Everyone else in the formation has their eyes shut.

Adaptations   Mark out three sides of a large enclosure on the floor. A shepherd tries to round up a group of blindfolded children (sheep) and move them into the pen one at a time using only four words – forwards, backwards, left, right – and a whistle to indicate the number of steps to take.

Players work in pairs and help their partner to 'explore' their surroundings through touch. They can progress from holding their partner's arm to touching an elbow, to just touching fingertips.

Reflection   What did you discover? What helped you to feel safe? Was it the reassurance of the leader? Precise directions? Tone of voice? Did you feel able to ask the leader to slow down if needed?

Notes

Sort us out

⑦
🕐 10 mins
♦ ♦ ♦
💬💬

☑ problem-solving ☑ categorization
☑ cooperation   ☑ asking questions
☑ memory   ☑ observation

How to play   The game coordinator times the group while they arrange themselves in a line according to one or more of the following criteria:

- alphabetically according to the first letter of their first name
- according to house number
- according to age
- according to what time they get up in the morning.

Adaptations   The children choose their own criteria for organizing the group into a line.

Smaller groups of children stand on a PE bench and then try to arrange themselves according to different criteria without stepping off the bench.

The game is played with criteria chosen that do not need any verbal interaction (e.g. height, groups of children with same eye colour or hair colour).

Imagine the room is divided into north, south, east and west. The children start off in the centre of the room and have to run and touch the appropriate wall when the game coordinator shouts out a category, e.g. 'brown eyes – west wall' or 'can ride a bike – east wall'.

Reflection   Which line took the least time to organize? Why? Which grouping took the longest? Why?

Think about similarities and differences and how we could be members of several different groups.

Notes

A very special tree

⑦
🕑 30 mins
👤 👤 👤
💬

☑ research skills
☑ imagination
☑ understanding
  similarities

☑ understanding
  characteristics
☑ understanding
  metaphors

How to play   Invite the children to draw a *very special tree* to show connections with their family.

Each child draws a tree shape and puts their own name or their photo or a 'self-portrait' on one of the branches and the names/photos of family members on all the other branches. Spend time colouring and decorating the trees, making them unique.

Display the trees on the wall.

Adaptations   Put the names of 'important people' on the branches instead of, or as well as, family members.

Instead of drawing trees, the children draw around their own hand and write the names of important people on each finger. This is their 'hand of friendship' or their 'helping hand' (people who are close to them and will help them if they get stuck).

Reflection   Talk about who is on each tree. Talk about what *sort* of tree each child has drawn. Is it an apple tree, a willow tree, a very ancient tree, a magic tree? Do not be tempted to interpret any of the drawings but do encourage older children to elaborate on the characteristics of their tree (strength, resilience, protective, small, new, wild, orderly, etc.). What are the similarities and differences between the children's trees?

Notes

Working parts

ⓖ   ☑ cooperation   ☑ creative thinking
🕐 15 mins   ☑ problem-solving ☑ observation
🕴 🕴 🕴   ☑ imagination
💬

You may need to brainstorm some ideas for machines with the group before you start the game (e.g. CD in a CD player, lawn mower, motorbike, computer with mouse, mobile phone).

How to play   Small teams (around five is a good number) think of a machine that has several working parts. Each member of the team takes on the role of a different part in the machine (and an 'operator'). Players can use sounds and actions and have parts working together or at different times.

Each team practises their machine and then demonstrates it for the other teams to guess what it is.

Adaptations   Teams pick a machine from a prepared set of cards.

Teams invent a machine and explain it to the rest of the group.

Reflection   Did all team members take an equal part? Is it possible for teams to be non-competitive? Did teams have a leader or did all members join in with the decision-making?

Notes

Sculptor

⑤
🕐 30 mins
🧍 🧍
💬💬

☑ listening
☑ cooperation
☑ imagination

☑ creative thinking
☑ awareness of others

Plenty of space is needed for this game.

How to play   Players take turns to be the 'sculptor' who creates an object by positioning the rest of the group. They can choose to create a snow ball, balloon, kite or boat.

Once they have sculpted the object they give instructions such as get bigger, go flat, fly high, fly fast, sway in the breeze, battle the storm, take me to a beautiful island, sink in the snow, pop! Each sculptor gives a maximum of five instructions.

Adaptation   Make a sculpture of a 'scene', e.g. objects in a park, garden, factory, or parts of the same static object.

Reflection   What did it feel like to be the sculptor?

What did it feel like to be part of the boat, the kite, etc.? How easy or difficult was it to follow instructions as a whole group? Did the sculptures follow a leader within the group?

Notes

Find the leader

⑤

🕐 10 mins

♦ ♦ ♦

♡

☑ non-verbal communication

☑ concentration
☑ observation

How to play   One person (the detective) leaves the room while the others choose a leader. The detective returns and stands in the middle of the circle. Players in the circle have to copy everything the leader does and the detective tries to spot who the leader is.

Adaptation   Have two leaders and two detectives. The leaders lead alternate players in the circle.

Reflection   How do leaders ensure they have the attention of the players? Does everyone watch the leader or is it sometimes a chain reaction? Talk about leading by example and leading by instruction.

Notes

How many feelings?

⑦
🕐 30 mins
† † †
♀♀♀

☑ empathy
☑ cooperation
☑ categorization

☑ negotiation
☑ trust

This game is about recognizing other people's feelings and noting similarities in feelings. You will need to make enough large wall charts for the number of groups playing plus one extra. Each chart should have four giant 'ladders' drawn on it – one for each emotional theme.

How to play   Groups are given a time limit in which to think of as many feeling words as possible within the four themes of anger, fear, sadness and joy. Each word is written on separate cards. Players in each group then decide between themselves where each emotion word should be placed on the ladders. For example 'furious' and 'annoyed' would be placed on the anger ladder but annoyed would be near the bottom of the ladder and furious would be higher up. Groups then combine to negotiate making a final wall chart to show all the emotions in an agreed order.

Adaptation   Mark out a long line on the floor to indicate a scale of one to ten. Groups of children choose a category and then each pick one of the emotion words from that category. They then arrange themselves in order of intensity along the line.

Reflection   Were there any disagreements about levels of emotions? Do some people experience emotions near the top of the ladders a lot of the time? How can we recognize different levels of similar emotions in ourselves and in others? Do we sometimes have a high-intensity emotion for low-intensity situations?

Notes

Big ball parachute game

⑤
🕐 10 mins
👤 👤 👤
💬

☑ cooperation
☑ concentration
☑ observation

This is just one of many possible ideas for a cooperative game using a parachute. If you have the space for groups to move freely it is well worth investing in a parachute and using it regularly for large group games.

How to play Players hold the parachute at waist level and send a very large ball around the circle. One half of the players aim to try and keep the ball in the circle while the other half try and send it out.

Adaptation Send several different sized balls around the circle, either with everyone cooperating to try to keep the balls going in the same direction or with half the group trying to send the balls out of the circle.

Reflection Talk about cooperating as a large group. What are some of the real-life situations where groups of children might need to cooperate? What happens when some members of the group are not cooperating?

Notes

Additional notes: more ideas for self and others games

Reflections

9

Feeling OK about being me

Foundation element: self-acceptance

Recognizing our achievements and being able to accept sincere praise and compliments is an important aspect of self-acceptance. This element also involves recognizing the areas that we can change or are already working on and those things that it would be much more difficult to change or may even be impossible to change.

Part of self-acceptance involves understanding the difference between making mistakes and failing. Young children are often not aware that older children and adults make mistakes too and that this can be a very productive way of learning – some of the most inspired inventors and scientists achieve their best creations through making mistakes in design and learning from them!

As discussed in the introductory chapters to this book, our self-concept includes all aspects of how we see ourselves, and self-acceptance therefore also includes body awareness and feeling OK about our physical appearance.

I like my hands because...

⑧
🕐 15 mins
👤 👤 👤
💬💬

☑ understanding characteristics
☑ creative thinking
☑ self-awareness

How to play   Each child draws round his or her own hand. In each finger they write why they like their hands, e.g. my hands are clever, creative, beautiful, strong, fast moving. In the palm they write one thing that their hands enable them to do – play the keyboard, cut up their food, stroke the cat.

Display the hand pictures for players to guess the artist.

Adaptations   Ask the children to 'introduce' their hands to the rest of the group and say
⑤   something about them.

Younger children can cut out magazine pictures to show things they like to do with their hands.

Make foot drawings and face drawings (using a mirror).

Reflection   Talk about differences and similarities. Do you take your hands for granted? Have you ever really looked at your hands very closely and noticed the patterns of lines, the skin colour, the way your fingers move?

Notes

Pass the shell

⑦

🕐 5 mins

👤 👤 👤

💬💬

☑ listening
☑ trust
☑ empathy

☑ taking turns
☑ giving and receiving
   praise

How to play   Use a large shell or a beautiful/unusual object of some sort. Pass the shell around the group. Whoever is holding it praises someone else and passes them the shell. This is best done in sequence around the circle to start with until you feel that children can praise each other in random order and not leave anyone out.

Adaptations   Each child has a piece of paper and writes their name at the bottom. The papers are passed around the group for everyone to write something positive about the person named on the paper. The paper is folded over after each comment has been added so that no one sees what anyone else has written. The paper is then returned to the original player to read.

Everyone has a piece of paper pinned to their back for others to write praises on.

Reflection   What does it feel like to give and receive praise? How many different ways can we praise each other? What would you most like to be praised for? What do you think your mother/brother/best friend would most like to be praised for? Is there anything you *don't* like to be praised for?

Notes

Three things about me

⑦
🕐 15 mins
👤 👤 👤
🗨🗨🗨

☑ trust
☑ asking questions
☑ taking turns

☑ initiating interactions
☑ respecting others

How to play	Players draw three things they are good at or really enjoy doing on a single sheet of paper. This is pinned to their front. Players walk around the room, looking at everyone else's drawings and talking about their pictures with each other.
Adaptations	Volunteers share their pictures in the circle.
	Pairs of children draw a picture or write one thing they think their partner is good at and pin it on their partner's back. Each child tries to find out what their 'skill' is by walking around the room and asking others questions such as 'Is it to do with a sport?' or 'Is it to do with friends?'
Reflection	Encourage children to explore the idea that everyone is good at some things and will find other things more difficult.
Notes	

Adverts

⑩

🕑 50 mins

† † †

◯◯◯

☑ creative thinking   ☑ understanding
☑ cooperation   characteristics
☑ planning   ☑ self-awareness

This game helps children to recognize and explore some of the skills and attributes they have in relation to different aspects of their lives.

How to play   Each player chooses a 'role' from a provided list. This could be a role that they actually play in life or one they would like to play. This works best if at least three children choose each role. Players are then grouped together according to their choices and cooperate to design a joint poster or TV advert for themselves in this particular role, highlighting skills and attributes. Volunteers share their posters in the circle.

Possible roles might be: sports ace, computer expert, brother/sister, son/daughter, friend, artist, science whizz-kid, inventor, builder.

Adaptation   Design 'your class needs you' posters highlighting attributes and skills needed for successful group work.

Reflection   Everyone has valuable skills and attributes.

Are the posters realistic? Do good friends always have all the identified attributes for example? Are our 'ideal' roles always achievable or are they sometimes unrealistic?

Notes

Building blocks

⑦
🕐 15 mins
† † †
💬

☑ self-awareness ☑ concentration
☑ cooperation   ☑ creative thinking

This game needs some preparation beforehand. You will need to find or draw a large picture of an imposing building such as a castle. Paste this onto card and then cut the picture into enough puzzle pieces to provide one piece for each child in the group.

How to play Players identify a skill that they are currently developing. They draw something to represent this skill on the back of a puzzle piece. When all players have completed a drawing the group tries to make the puzzle in a given time limit. This can either be done by using the picture or by shape alone. Tape the pieces together so that either side of the finished puzzle can be displayed.

Adaptation Use large plastic bricks or bricks drawn on card to build a structure (wall, house, school, etc.) with different assets on each brick or different things of which children are proud.

Reflection Discuss learning 'sets' of skills and building up abilities gradually. Compare this to having a natural ability which might need to be practised and developed (such as singing). Are there some skills that everyone needs? Are there any skills that most of us don't need?

Notes

'Eye' spy

⑦
🕐 10 mins
🧍 🧍 🧍
🗨🗨🗨

☑ respecting others   ☑ eye contact
☑ observation   ☑ trust
☑ taking turns

How to play   Players walk around the room and meet each other. Each time they meet up with someone they stay and look at each other's eyes for at least one minute, taking turns to describe exactly what the other person's eyes look like – not just the main colour but as many other details as possible.

Adaptation   Children use mirrors to draw their own eyes and colour them in with as much detail as possible. The group tries to guess the owners of the drawings.

Reflection   Why is eye contact important when we communicate with each other? What do you like about your eyes? When you walk do you look down at the ground most of the time or do you look around you? What messages do our eyes give to others?

Notes

Magic monkey dance

⑤
🕐 10 mins
🧍 🧍 🧍
💬

☑ empathy   ☑ self-control
☑ self-awareness   ☑ observation
☑ taking turns

How to play   One player takes the part of the magician. The magician is able to cast a spell to make children dance like monkeys and to make them freeze. The rest of the group is divided into two halves – rescuers and dancers. Rescuers stand in a wide circle. The dancers move around the centre of the circle in time to music. When the magician stops the music the dancers freeze in whatever position they are in. The rescuers must take turns to exactly copy the position of one of the dancers. When a dancer thinks their rescuer has got it exactly right they are saved and can unfreeze and sit down around the edge of the group. The game coordinator may need to help some children to closely mirror positions. The rescuers must stay frozen until every dancer has been saved. Then the magician has lost his or her powers. A new magician is chosen, the rescuers and dancers swap over and the music starts again.

Adaptations   Choose animals that have different ways of moving, for example snakes, birds, crocodiles (with arms stretched out to make the crocodile's jaws).

Rescued dancers can help other rescuers.

Reflection   How easy or difficult is it to stay completely still? How easy or difficult is it to try and mirror someone else's posture? Did you need to look at your own hand shape, etc. to see if your rescuer got it right or did you just 'sense' your posture?

Notes

Colourful me

⑧　　　　　　　　　☑ creative thinking
🕐 20 mins　　　　　☑ self-awareness
👤 👤 👤　　　　　　☑ understanding metaphors
💬

You will need to collect enough see-through plastic jars or bottles for each person to have their own (small plastic water bottles are ideal) and lots of different materials, e.g. glitter, sand, beads, coloured rice, lentils, flour – the more varied the colours, the better.

How to play　Each child makes a container of talents and assets and things they like about themselves. Fill the container with layers of different materials or different colours of the same material, one layer to represent each talent, etc. (so layers may be of different thicknesses). Label the top of the container. It doesn't matter if some children end up shaking the container and mixing everything up. Obviously there will be some 'settling' of materials as well and some things will shift. Display the containers on shelves.

Adaptations　Draw a jar and colour in different shapes and layers in the jar.

Make a container for things you appreciate about someone else and present it to them.

Make a jar for things you're working on.

Draw a 'key' to what's in the jar or write an ingredients label.

Reflection　Discuss the importance of enjoying our talents and appreciating our different qualities. Note the uniqueness of the containers. Talk about how things change and shift.

Notes

Important names

⑦
🕐 5 mins
🧍 🧍 🧍
💬

☑ listening
☑ self-awareness
☑ taking turns

☑ respecting others
☑ understanding
   characteristics

I use a Tibetan bell for the adapted version of this game. Children ring it just once and say their name as the chime resonates around the room. It can add a wonderful sense of grandeur and dignity to the sound of each name.

How to play   Each child chooses a special word to describe herself, beginning with the first letter of her name (e.g. energetic Erin, happy Hilary). Stand in a circle and use a softball or beanbag to throw. On the first round the catcher says her own special name. On the second round the thrower calls out another child's special name as she throws the ball/beanbag to her.

Adaptations
⑤
Children choose special names to reflect particular talents (not necessarily using the first letter of their name).

Use a small bell with a clapper. The first player carries the bell slowly across the circle to another child, trying not to let it ring. The child who receives the bell rings it loudly and says (or shouts!) their special name (younger children can just say their first name). They then carry the bell across the circle to another child and so on until everyone has had a turn.

Reflection   Think about the enjoyment of saying and hearing your own name. How can you celebrate your name? Take time to reflect on the qualities in yourself that you really like. Why is self-respect important? How do we show self-respect and respect for others?

Notes

Puppets

⑤   ☑ self-awareness   ☑ empathy
🕐 **5 mins**   ☑ self-control   ☑ concentration
♀ ♀ ♀
♀

There are so many body awareness games that involve movement
that it was hard to pick just one! However, I do want to emphasize
how important it is for children to experience the way in which their
body moves and how they can have different degrees of control over
movement. Understanding how the body works and what it is capable
of is a great step towards building this area of self-esteem.

How to play   Tell the children that they are going to pretend to be puppets. They start in a
standing position with their feet firmly on the ground, their arms stretched
upwards and fingers spread out as though they are being held up by strings.
They imagine that the strings are very slowly being loosened so that their
body starts to drop down. Start with just the fingers, then hands, arms, head
and upper body, finally bending slightly at the knees. The same movements
are then performed in reverse until the children are standing upright again
with arms stretched as high as they can. Do this several times at varying
speeds.

Adaptation   In pairs take turns at being puppet and puppeteer. Without touching the
puppet the puppeteer pretends to pull strings to get different parts of the
puppet to move in different directions and at different speeds. This works
well if the puppet is lying down to start with and the puppeteer has to work
out which strings to pull in order to get the puppet to stand up.

Reflection   How does your body move? What aspects of movements can you control
(speed, direction, range)? Think about the complicated sequence of movements needed to stand up or sit down. How do we learn how to do this? Talk
about how children make mistakes and fall over when they are learning but as
we get older we move without thinking about it. Can you tell when your
muscles are relaxed and when they are tense? Do you ever think about your
shoulders, your back, the backs of your knees?!

Notes

Additional notes: more ideas for self-acceptance games

Reflections

10

Taking care of myself

Foundation element: self-reliance

Of course, the skills needed to build self-reliance are acquired very gradually in childhood, but each step can be a tremendous boost to self-esteem, especially if they are noted and celebrated.

A child's physical achievements such as being able to dress himself or ride a bike are often acknowledged and celebrated, but there are other areas of self-reliance which may be missed by both the child and by adults as well. These small triumphs of emotional self-care can be a powerful force for increased motivation, independent thinking, self-efficacy and emotional resilience and we need to be on the look-out for them and encourage them just as much as the physical signs of self-reliance.

When children start to develop a degree of self-reliance they are more able to enjoy the exciting and fun things in life and more ready to cope with things that are challenging or difficult.

Pass a smile

⑤

🕐 5 mins

☝ ☝ ☝

🗨

☑ taking turns
☑ concentration
☑ self-awareness

☑ observation
☑ non-verbal
    communication

How to play   Players sit in a circle. Everyone tries to look very solemn. A child is chosen to start off a smile. He sends a smile to the person sitting next to him. This person smiles then 'zips' their lips in order to 'hold' the smile. He then turns to the next person and unzips the smile to pass it on! When the smile has been around the circle once, the group have a go at passing another smile but this time even more quickly.

Adaptation   'Throw' a smile across the circle. Everyone has to stay on the alert to catch it!

Reflection   Talk about how it is possible to sometimes have control over how we feel. How does your body feel when you smile? What makes you smile? Can you tell the difference between a genuine smile and a pretend one or an 'unkind' smile? *How* can you tell the difference?

Notes

Melting snowman

⑤   ☑ imagination   ☑ self-monitoring
🕐 5 mins   ☑ self-awareness   ☑ dramatic awareness
♀ ♀ ♀
♡

How to play   Spread out around the room so that each child has plenty of space in which to 'melt'. Start by imagining that you are a newly-built snowman. Stand very still with your arms by your side. Make all your muscles quite tense. Now imagine the sun has come out and it is getting warmer and warmer. Feel yourself 'melt' until you are a pool of melted snow on the floor. Lie very still, letting all your muscles go floppy. Now the snow clouds come and lots of snow falls so that you can be built up into a snowman again. Melt once more. Then you are back to being you. Stand up tall. Shake your hands and arms and legs as if you are shaking the snow off. Feel the strength in your body.

Adaptation   Alternate between being a rag doll and a wooden or metal toy.

Reflection   What does it feel like to be tense and what does it feel like to be very relaxed? Notice the difference between being very tense as a snowman and feeling strong without feeling excessive tension. Why is it important for our bodies to be relaxed sometimes? Is there such a thing as useful tension? When do we need to be tense? Are there times when you have tension in your body that doesn't need to be there?

Notes

Worry stories

⑧
🕑 **50 mins**
🧍 🧍 🧍
🗨🗨🗨

☑ listening   ☑ dramatic awareness
☑ cooperation   ☑ sequencing/story-telling
☑ planning

How to play   Make a group list of things that children might worry about at school or when playing with friends. Small groups of children are invited to make up a short story about 'the day the worries took over our school'. They practise this together, taking an equal share in the telling. The groups then take turns to tell their story to the whole group.

Adaptation   Groups make up a short play involving a detective who has been sent to a small town where worries have taken over all the adults. The detective interviews a teacher, a doctor, a baker, a firefighter, a factory worker, a builder, etc. Each person is *very* worried about everything to do with their job!

Reflection   Do you think everyone has worries? Do people worry about the same sorts of things? Are some worries useful? What happens when worries take up a lot of thinking time and aren't resolved? Who do you share worries with? What could you do with your worries?

Notes

I packed my suitcase

⑧
🕒 5 mins
⛉ ⛉ ⛉
💬💬

☑ listening
☑ memory
☑ taking turns

☑ creative thinking
☑ categorization

This is a familiar memory game adapted to help children to think carefully about what they might need for different situations.

How to play
Brainstorm a variety of different activities or adventures that would need different equipment and clothing as well as items that would be relevant for any situation (e.g. mountaineering, deep-sea diving, going to an adventure playground, visiting a hot country, visiting a cold country, going on a treasure hunt).

Choose one of these and play a round of 'I packed my suitcase and I took…'. Each child has to remember what has already been packed and add one more item to the list. When the list gets too long to remember, choose another adventure and start again.

Adaptation
Older children can challenge the inclusion of an item that doesn't seem relevant for the particular adventure.

Reflection
How can we prepare ourselves for adventures and challenges? If we think something is going to be scary, embarrassing or difficult what could we do to help ourselves to cope with this?

Notes

Run like the wind

⑤
🕐 5 mins
🧍 🧍 🧍
💬

☑ listening   ☑ imagination
☑ self-awareness   ☑ self-control
☑ observation

How to play	Explain to the children that you are the head of a village in the jungle and you are in charge of looking after all the village children while they play. They are an extremely noisy group of children and run like the wind through the jungle, shouting and laughing. The only danger in the jungle is lions! You can hear the lions coming long before the children can. They have to watch you carefully and when you sit down with your hand over your mouth they have to sit down immediately too. Their silence and stillness will trick the lions, who will go away. You signal that the danger is passed by shouting 'run like the wind!'. Then everyone gets up and runs and shouts again.
Adaptation	Choose new village leaders in a way that no-one else knows who has been chosen.
Reflection	How easy or difficult is it to stay aware of what is going on when you are doing something very active?
	Talk about the importance of having a mixture of active times and quiet times.
Notes	

Sleeping monsters

⑤   ☑ self-awareness
🕐 5 mins   ☑ self-control
👤 👤 👤
💬

This is a very slight adaptation of the familiar game of 'Sleeping lions'.

How to play   The monsters are stamping around the room with heavy footsteps until they are suddenly very tired and have to lie down on the ground and close their eyes. The game coordinator walks quietly around the room to see if they are all really asleep. The coordinator can talk but must not touch the monsters. If any monsters are seen to move then they must get up and help to spot any others who are moving.

Adaptation   Use two different types of music – one very loud with a heavy beat and one quiet and gentle. The monsters move to the sound of the first and lie down when they hear the second.

Reflection   Does your breathing change when you are being calm? How does it change? When might it be useful to make your breathing calm on purpose?

Notes

Shake it out

⑦
🕐 10 mins
† † †
◯◯

☑ self-awareness ☑ taking turns
☑ creative thinking ☑ trust

How to play   Make a list of 'difficult' feelings (e.g. anger, sadness, jealousy, frustration, being fed-up). Brainstorm ideas for what to do with these feelings (e.g. when I feel angry I can tell someone, do something active to get rid of the tension in my body, scribble in a scribble book, etc.).

Do rounds of 'I feel angry when…', etc. After each round, end with a shake to release any tension. Everyone shakes their arms and legs and shoulders. Finish with a round of 'When difficult feelings come I know how to…'.

Adaptation   Each child pretends their fingers are having a mock fight, scrabbling around
⑤   each other moving very fast, clasping hands together, feeling the tightness. Now change to 'floating' fingers, gently and slowly moving around each other, one hand stroking the other. Change back and forth two or three times and then eventually hands float down to rest in the child's lap.

Reflection   Difficult feelings come and go. Feelings don't last for ever. Just because we might feel angry now doesn't mean that we are always going to be an angry person. These feelings are normal. It is good to know how to handle them.

Notes

Circle move

⑤

🕓 5 mins

👤 👤 👤

💬

☑ self-awareness   ☑ concentration
☑ eye contact   ☑ observation
☑ taking turns

How to play   Players sit in a circle. One child starts off a movement such as a shoulder shake. Each child copies this in turn until everyone is making the same movement. Then everyone stops in turn until the circle is still. The person sitting to the left of the first player then starts a different movement and sends this around the group in the same way. Do this as many times as feels comfortable, varying the speed.

Adaptations   Two players sitting on opposite sides of the circle start off two different movements at the same time and send them in the same direction or in opposite directions.

Players 'throw' the movement to each other across the circle by gaining eye contact with another player.

Reflection   Being active can help us to feel good. A short period of exercise can help us to concentrate more easily. What sort of exercise do you enjoy?

Notes

Giggle switch

⑤
🕐 5 mins
👤 👤 👤
💬

☑ self-awareness   ☑ taking turns
☑ self-control   ☑ eye contact

How to play   Pairs sit facing each other. They choose who is A and who is B. They must keep eye contact and try to keep a straight face. The game coordinator waits until everyone is quiet and then says 'giggle switch', at which point person A tries to make person B giggle in any way they can without touching them. At any point the coordinator can say 'giggle switch' again and the players have to swap roles.

Adaptation   The children lie down on the floor in a circle with heads nearly touching in the centre and feet facing towards the outside of the circle, their hands resting gently on their stomachs. The first person starts off by saying 'ha!', the second says 'ha ha!', the third says 'ha ha ha!', and so on, going as fast as possible until someone starts to laugh for real. Then everyone has to wait for silence before another child starts off a round of 'ho!'. This can also be played with each child lying with their head on someone else's stomach. The movement involved in saying 'ha!' can cause laughter before the round gets very far at all!

Reflection   Talk about the importance of laughter. How do you feel when you have had a 'fit of the giggles'? Talk about the difference between 'laughing at someone' and 'laughing with someone'. Laughter can have very different qualities and can therefore cause us to *feel* quite different physically.

Notes

Bravery awards

⑤   ☑ self-awareness   ☑ respecting others
🕐 5 mins   ☑ trust   ☑ giving and receiving
👤 👤 👤   ☑ taking turns   praise
💬

How to play   Talk about times when we do something a *little bit* scary that might take some
courage. Suggest very 'ordinary' situations (e.g. first day at a new school,
learning to ride a bike, diving into the pool for the first time, reading aloud in
the school play). Encourage children to think up at least ten situations. Now
brainstorm ways in which we acknowledge someone else's bravery. This
could be verbal praise, thumbs up, clapping, etc. or a full award ceremony. Do
a round of 'I was brave when…' with each child choosing one situation from
the list. The rest of the group acknowledge the child's bravery noisily and
enthusiastically!

Adaptation   Acknowledge small triumphs of mastery; times of making a 'wise decision';
times of solving a problem.

Reflection   Talk about learning to notice our own small achievements and praising
ourselves. Sometimes other people don't notice or don't know how we feel
or what we've achieved. Just because they don't praise us doesn't mean that
we didn't do well.

Notes

Additional notes: more ideas for self-reliance games

Reflections

11

More than just talking

Foundation element: self-expression

This chapter is concerned with how we communicate with each other through our body language, facial expression and tone of voice as well as the words we use.

Learning to 'read' other people's non-verbal communication is a skill which some children have difficulty in mastering. This can be particularly difficult for children if the significant people in their lives are ambiguous in their messages of affection and chastisement.

Self-expression is also about recognizing and celebrating the unique ways in which we each express who we are.

Emotions

⑤
🕐 5 mins
👤 👤 👤
💬

☑ dramatic
  awareness
☑ imagination

☑ non-verbal
  communication
☑ self-awareness

How to play   The game coordinator suggests different emotions and all members of the group try to show these emotions in any non-verbal way they like, for example as an animal, as a movement, by facial expression or the way they walk. The coordinator shouts 'freeze' and everyone 'holds' the pose and feels what it's like for a few seconds.

Shake that feeling out of the body (shake arms, hands, legs). Then try a different emotion. Finish with at least two positive emotions.

Adaptation   Act out actions and feelings together randomly, e.g. doing the ironing sadly, eating a sandwich angrily.

Reflection   Sometimes we can be saying one thing and feeling something completely different. Does our body language sometimes 'give the game away'? If someone tells you they are angry but they are smiling would you believe their words or their facial expression?

Notes

If hands could talk

⑨
🕐 5 mins
† † †
◯

☑ dramatic awareness
☑ imagination

☑ non-verbal communication
☑ self-awareness

How to play   Ask the children to stand in a large enough space so that they have room to move their arms and hands without touching other people. Demonstrate how we can move our arms freely in the air and at the same time shake our hands loosely. When all the children are moving freely call 'freeze'. From this frozen position each child is then told to let one hand fall by their side and to look carefully at the one that is still in mid-air. What name could be given to this 'frozen' gesture? Ask the children to change their hand position slightly. What name would they give to this new gesture? Each person then invents a 'hand dance' changing from one gesture to the other and back again.

Adaptations   Try the hand dances at different speeds and to different types of music.

Children work together in pairs or threes to combine their hand dances and then demonstrate to the rest of the group.

Try the same sequence of free movement, freezing and changing using whole body movements and giving names to the different postures.

Reflection   Talk about how even subtle changes in body language can make a big difference to how we feel and to how other people *think* we feel. Can you think of postures that look nearly the same but mean something very different?

Notes

If feelings were colours

⑤
🕐 10 mins
👤 👤 👤
💬

☑ empathy
☑ imagination
☑ observation

☑ dramatic awareness
☑ non-verbal
　communication

How to play　The game coordinator leads a very brief discussion about how different feelings could be thought of as different colours. For example, 'I'm the colour blue today because I feel calm'; 'I'm the colour blue today because I feel sad'; 'I'm the colour red because I feel full of energy'. Ask the children what colour they would be today and why they would be that colour. The children then try to 'feel' what it is like to move around the room as this colour.

Adaptations　Everyone tries the same colour. Do the movements first and then ask what emotion/feeling the children had when they moved as this colour.

Try three or four different colours in succession.

Groups of children choose a colour to portray to the rest of the group who have to guess which colour it is.

Reflection　Do all the blues move in the same way? How do different colours move? Is it easy to change from one 'mood' to another? When might that happen?

Notes

Feel it, do it

⑦
🕐 5 mins
👤 👤 👤
🗨

☑ self-awareness   ☑ dramatic awareness
☑ empathy   ☑ observation
☑ taking turns

How to play   Players stand in a circle facing each other. Volunteers take turns to take one
step into the circle and show with their whole body the way that they are
feeling today. Then they say their name (in a way that also reflects the
emotion) and step back. The whole group steps forward and reflects back the
action and the original person's name. Everyone steps back. The next
volunteer steps forward. Players do not need to name the emotions.

Adaptation   Players start by crouching down low. Volunteers 'pop' up and then crouch
down again when they have shown their feeling and said their name. The
whole group 'pops' up to reflect the feeling and then crouches down to wait
for the next volunteer.

Reflection   Do you ever have feelings that you don't understand or don't know why you
feel that way? Do people show the same emotions in different ways?

Notes

Hide and seek

⑥
🕐 5 mins
👤 👤 👤
💬

☑ self-awareness
☑ self-control
☑ observation

☑ non-verbal
communication

How to play
One player leaves the room. The group throws a small soft ball or beanbag across the circle to each other until the player outside knocks on the door loudly three times before coming in. Whoever has the ball or beanbag at that point has to hide it quickly. The first player has to look carefully at the facial expression and body language of all the players to try and guess who has the object. Three guesses are allowed before a second player has a go.

Adaptation
A bead or a ring is threaded onto one long piece of string. The group holds the string lightly in their hands (palms facing downwards) and passes the ring around the circle until the player outside knocks on the door and comes in. All hands are then held at waist height so the person guessing can only go by facial expression or pure chance to find who is holding the ring.

Reflection
What are the main facial expressions that everyone recognizes? Which part of the face is the most expressive part? Eyes? Mouth? Nose? Forehead?

Notes

Follow my walk

⑦
🕐 10 mins
♪ ♪ ♪
💬

☑ empathy
☑ trust
☑ self-awareness

☑ observation
☑ giving and accepting
   compliments

How to play   Players stand or sit in a circle. A volunteer walks across the circle several times. The group members give positive comments about the way that the volunteer walked. For example, 'You held your head up; you looked well balanced; you smiled; your shoulders were relaxed.' Then everyone tries to walk in exactly the same way to really feel what it is like to walk like this person.

Have as many volunteers as possible and reassure everyone that they will get a go at another time if they want to.

Adaptation   Imagine a character role and try to walk as you think they would walk, e.g. the strongest person in the world, an old person, someone who has just been told some good news.

Reflection   How does our walk express how we feel about ourselves? What parameters can be changed (e.g. walking with light/heavy footsteps; large strides/small steps; slowly/quickly; with a 'bounce'; arms swinging/arms stiff)?

Notes

Talking heads

⑨
🕐 10 mins

☑ listening   ☑ concentration
☑ cooperation   ☑ anticipation
☑ taking turns

How to play   In pairs, children put one arm round each other and act as if they were one person. They talk about a given subject with each person saying one word at a time to make sentences. This means that they have to guess what the other person is aiming to say and it can get quite frustrating and difficult! Topics could include 'Why I like chocolate', 'What I did yesterday', 'My favourite holiday', 'What I learned at school this morning'.

Adaptation   The audience ask questions and the pair have to answer one word at a time.

Reflection   Did pairs manage to cooperate to make sense even if they couldn't guess what their partner was going to say? Sometimes we think we know what other people are thinking. Sometimes we expect others to know what *we* are thinking!

Notes

This is me

⑦
🕐 10 mins
👤 👤
💬💬

☑ dramatic
   awareness
☑ self-awareness
☑ observation

☑ understanding
   characteristics
☑ non-verbal
   communication

How to play   Make a group list of positive words that can be used to describe a person's character, e.g. careful, friendly, creative. Write each one on a separate card. Now brainstorm at least ten actions and write each of these on separate cards as well.

Players take turns to pick an action and a characteristic from the two piles of cards and attempt to do the action in the manner of the characteristic, e.g. brush your hair carefully; stroke a dog in a friendly way; wave creatively! The rest of the group try to guess the characteristic.

Adaptations   In larger groups children perform the actions in teams of threes or fours for everyone else to guess.

Each child chooses one or more words from the list that could be used to describe their own personality. If you have already played 'Figure me out!' (page 52) they might like to add these words to their collage.

Reflection   Do we show our main characteristics in everything we do?

Do we show our main characteristics through action only?

What three positive things would your best friend say about you? Would they be right?

Notes

Mirror talking

⑤
🕐 5 mins
👤 👤 👤
💬

☑ self-awareness   ☑ observation
☑ empathy   ☑ non-verbal
☑ trust   communication

How to play | Children sit opposite each other in pairs and take turns to mirror each other's hand movements as closely as possible.

Adaptations | Use music to evoke different moods for the hand movements.

Give a theme beforehand.

Reflection | How easy or difficult was this? What skills are needed in order to follow someone else's gestures in this way? Do you use your hands much when you talk? Do you know anyone who uses *lots* of gesture when talking? Do you know anyone who hardly moves their hands at all? Do you normally notice gesture? Watch a soap opera on TV and report back on which character gestures the most.

Notes

Variety show

⑩

🕐 **30 mins**

🧍 🧍 🧍

💬

☑ self-awareness   ☑ self-respect
☑ trust   ☑ dramatic awareness
☑ creative thinking

Players will need to have plenty of preparation time before this game.

How to play
Invite the children (volunteers) to take turns in showing the rest of the group something that creatively expresses a positive aspect of how they see themselves. This can be an object chosen from home (such as a blanket, a floaty silk scarf, a favourite toy); a short piece of music (drum beats, a well-known song); a drawing; a dance; a single movement; a short story; a poem – absolutely anything at all! There is no interpretation needed unless the children want to explain the relevance of an object they have chosen. The children each give their presentation and the group respond with applause and praise.

Adaptation
Players choose something they are wearing or something they have with them on the day (i.e. no preparation) and say in what way it reflects their own personality.

Reflection
Think of as many ways as possible that we show how we are feeling/our personality.

Notes

Personal interviews

⑦
🕒 10 mins
♟ ♟ ♟
💬

☑ listening   ☑ taking turns
☑ empathy   ☑ trust
☑ asking questions

How to play   Drape a chair with a brightly coloured blanket or cloth. Children take turns to sit in the chair and are interviewed by the rest of the group. Questions can be about their likes and dislikes, wishes, holidays, favourite books, pet hates, etc. or they can be interviewed about a particular interest they have.

Adaptation   Use two chairs, one for the person being interviewed and one for volunteer interviewers who can come and sit in the chair and ask one question before returning to their place in the audience.

Reflection   How does it feel to have the chance to talk about yourself? How does 'being interviewed' compare to having a conversation with someone? Talk about taking turns in conversations and asking questions to show a genuine interest in the other person. What does it feel like when a friend asks you questions about yourself?

Notes

Additional notes: more ideas for self-expression games

Reflections

12

Solving problems

Foundation element: self-confidence

Self-confidence involves developing our knowledge and abilities so that we feel able to experiment with different methods of problem-solving and can be flexible enough to alter strategies if needed.

We all have creative potential but many of us fail to use it constructively. The amount of creativity we use is closely related to our self-concept.

As children learn to tolerate the frustration of making mistakes and begin to experience success they start to trust in their own judgements and decisions more and more. This helps to confirm their abilities and self-worth and gives them confidence to know that they will be able to cope with future difficulties effectively.

Create that!

⑨   ☑ imagination   ☑ dramatic awareness
🕐 **5 mins**   ☑ creative thinking ☑ non-verbal
🧍 🧍 🧍   ☑ observation   communication
💬

How to play   Players stand in a circle. The game coordinator mimes taking off a hat and passes this imaginary object to player A. This player changes the hat into something else (e.g. a mixing bowl or a toy boat) and mimes using it/playing with it, before passing it on to player B. When the object has been all round the circle the game coordinator takes it back and wears it as a hat again. Players must attempt to make the transformations from one object to another connect up in some way.

Adaptation   Pass the same imaginary object around the circle for each player to use in a different way.

Reflection   Think about having fun while solving problems. Sometimes there is not a right and a wrong way of doing things – there are just different ways!

Notes

Musical balance

⑦
🕐 5 mins
👤 👤 👤
💬

☑ listening
☑ cooperation

☑ trust
☑ self-awareness

How to play

Players form a circle with each person holding on to the waist of the person in front of them. They walk around while music is playing. When the music stops they have to sit down gently on the lap of the person behind them. The circle usually collapses the first few times but most groups can eventually manage this very successfully.

Adaptation

Play musical chairs, but instead of players being 'out' when chairs are removed, they can balance on another person's lap so there will be more and more people sitting on each chair and they will have to balance carefully.

Reflection

It's OK to make mistakes or for things to not quite work out. By persevering and altering the way we approach the task or by improving our skills we can often solve the problem. Does this game involve a problem or a challenge?

Notes

Abandon ship!

⑨
🕐 **30 mins**
♦ ♦ ♦
◯◯◯

☑ negotiation
☑ compromise
☑ cooperation

☑ creative thinking
☑ problem-solving

How to play   Split into an equal number of small groups or pairs, according to the size of the whole group. Within each group members imagine that they are on a ship that is about to sink. They have a lifeboat but they are only allowed to take ten items with them from the ship. First they think of ten items each. They then have to negotiate with other team members as to what to take as they can only take ten items between them. Groups then join with another group and renegotiate the ten items. Eventually the whole group meet and negotiate a final ten items.

Adaptation   The whole group has been shipwrecked. They have two empty plastic bottles to use on the desert island. Small groups or pairs think of as many uses as possible for the two bottles. The whole group then pool their ideas.

Reflection   How did it feel? Is everyone happy with the final decision? Is everyone happy with how the negotiations went? Did everyone get a chance to put their ideas forward? In the final group did a clear leader emerge? How easy or difficult was it to agree on ten items? What are some of the benefits of working in a group to solve problems?

Notes

Criss-cross parachute game

⑤
🕐 10 mins
👤 👤 👤
💬

☑ listening   ☑ trust
☑ cooperation   ☑ self-awareness

How to play   Players squat down, holding the edges of the parachute at ground level. The game coordinator says '1, 2, 3 parachute' or '1, 2, 3 sky-high' and everyone stands up with arms above their heads to inflate the parachute. The coordinator then quickly gives an instruction for children to cross beneath the parachute while it is still up in the air. For example 'Everyone who had cereal for breakfast', 'Everyone who is wearing black shoes'. Players then take turns to give instructions (either volunteering or in turn around the circle).

Adaptation   Players take turns to give instructions for moving the parachute in different ways at ground level (e.g. like ripples on a pond, like great waves, like a sheet of ice) while two or more players walk across the surface in an appropriate way to match the motion.

Reflection   Talk about 'thinking on your feet' and acting quickly. Talk about having the confidence to give instructions.

Notes

Good news and bad news

⑧
🕐 5 mins

☑ creative thinking
☑ understanding opposites
☑ concentration

☑ understanding consequences
☑ sequencing/story-telling

How to play   Players sit in a circle. The game coordinator starts off with a piece of 'good' news. The next person adds 'but the bad news is…'. For example 'the good news is that school is closed for the day…the bad news is that we all have extra homework to do. The good news is that the homework is to write about the local funfair…the bad news is that the funfair is closed for repairs…the good news is that the owner of the funfair is giving away free ice cream…the bad news is that they don't have any cones.'

Adaptations   Play this in pairs with a strict time limit.

Keep the good and bad news related to a single theme such as the weather or bathing the dog.

Reflection   Talk about being creative in thinking up possible good news related to the 'bad' news. Have you ever been in a difficult situation that turned out to be useful for you?

Notes

Tangled up

⑤
🕐 5 mins
👤 👤 👤
💬

☑ problem-solving ☑ self-awareness
☑ cooperation   ☑ observation
☑ creative thinking

A well-known problem-solving game which children never seem to tire of playing!

How to play   The whole group joins hands to form a chain. The person at one end begins to weave in and out, leading other members into a 'tangle' without breaking the links. Players can go over/under arms; between legs, etc. Two people then try to untangle the group by giving instructions only. They cannot touch the chain at all.

Adaptation   Children stand in a circle then close their eyes and stretch out their hands to find other hands. They then open their eyes and try to untangle themselves without letting go.

Reflection   How did it feel to be in the role of problem-solver?

               What were the important things to remember so that the chain did not break and no one got hurt? Have you ever come across problems that seemed too complex to unravel at first? How should we tackle that sort of problem?

Notes

Story challenge

⑩
🕐 20 mins
👤 👤 👤
💬 💬 💬

☑ cooperation
☑ memory
☑ non-verbal
    communication

☑ observation
☑ dramatic awareness
☑ imagination

It is important that the players don't know what sequences have been given to other teams.

How to play

Divide the group into smaller teams of three or four players. Each team is given a short non-verbal sequence to practise such as putting up a tent, hanging out the washing on a very windy day, catching a dog and giving it a bath. One team silently demonstrates their sequence to the rest of the group. A second team is then chosen to repeat what they have just seen and add their own dialogue. Continue until all the teams have done their own sequence and put dialogue to another team's sequence.

Adaptation

Groups are told that they are going to tell a story using objects collected from outside or from the room (one object for each person). They are given ten minutes to collect their objects and think of a theme for their story. Instead of telling their own story, however, each group then swaps objects with another group who tell an *unrehearsed* story with each person taking an equal part.

Reflection

Talk about working in a group to deal with the unexpected.

Talk about misunderstanding non-verbal signals.

What does it feel like when someone changes your story (either another group or someone within your own group)?

Notes

Guess what?!

⑦
🕐 10 mins
🧍 🧍 🧍
💬

☑ imagination
☑ deduction

☑ dramatic awareness
☑ observation

How to play
Provide a prop for children to use in different ways. The rest of the group have to guess what it is (e.g. a small mat used as a wheelchair, a seat of a car, a shield, a cloak or rolled up as a sword).

You might want to brainstorm a few ideas first or just let children step forward as soon as they think of something.

Adaptation
Provide two or three props that have to be combined together by pairs of children in a spontaneous cooperative mime.

Reflection
Talk about being spontaneous. Often it is good to plan ahead but sometimes we can over-plan things and get anxious about something long before it ever happens.

Notes

Additional notes: more ideas for self-confidence games

Reflections

13

All my senses

Foundation element: self-awareness

Self-awareness involves being able to identify our emotions and understand the reasons why we feel the way we do in different situations. It also involves an awareness of the way in which our thoughts can affect us physically.

In order to be constructively self-aware children need to be able to concentrate and focus on what their senses are telling them, noting changes and recognizing that they have some control over the way that they feel and behave.

Sense tracking

⑥

🕐 10 mins

♦ ♦ ♦

◯◯

☑ categorization   ☑ taking turns
☑ memory   ☑ observation
☑ deduction

How to play   The game coordinator provides a tray of different foods and items with a variety of different textures, sounds and smells (at least 20 items). The whole group is shown the tray uncovered for 30 seconds. The tray is then covered with a cloth and the first person looks under the cloth and starts off the game, naming any sense as appropriate:

- I spy with my little eye something beginning with…

- I hear with my little ear…

- I smell with my little nose…

- I feel with my little hands…

- I taste with my little tongue…

Whoever guesses correctly takes the next turn.

Of course, the game gets easier, the longer it is played, as people begin to remember what is under the cloth.

Adaptation   Play the game outside, referring to all the senses to guess things in the environment.

Reflection   Which sense do you think you use the most? When you close your eyes for a while do you hear sounds that you hadn't noticed before (e.g. the clock ticking)?

Notes

Sleeping bear

⑤
🕐 5 mins
🧍 🧍 🧍
💬

☑ listening
☑ waiting
☑ self-monitoring

A game to heighten concentration and listening skills.

How to play | The game coordinator chooses the first person to be the bear. This person sits on a chair in the middle of the circle or at the far end of the room, blind-folded. A bunch of keys is placed under the chair. The game coordinator chooses a player to creep up to the chair and steal the keys before the bear can point at him or her. If they manage to get the keys then he or she becomes the new bear.

Adaptation | Two children at a time cross the room from opposite ends. They both keep their eyes shut. One is the hunter and one is the bear. They must both move slowly and cautiously and listen out for each other.

Reflection | Talk about self-control and self-monitoring. Talk about the difference between listening with full attention and hearing noises without fully attending.

Notes

All change

⑥

🕐 5 mins

👤 👤 👤

💬

☑ memory

☑ waiting

☑ awareness of others

☑ observation

How to play   One player leaves the room. Someone in the group changes something about herself (e.g. removes her shoes, puts on a jumper, or ties her hair back). The observer returns and tries to guess who has changed and what they have changed.

Adaptation   Two children leave the room. Three people change something physically or change places and the two players have to say what the changes are.

Reflection   Talk about observation skills and looking with full awareness as opposed to just 'glancing' at something. Why do we need to be selective in what we pay attention to at any one time?

Notes

Musical drawings

⑦
🕐 20 mins

☑ listening
☑ imagination

☑ self-confidence
☑ concentration

How to play   The game coordinator plays a variety of music and the group draws whatever comes to mind while listening to the different rhythms and moods.

Adaptation   Children bring in their own selections of music and talk about how they feel when they listen to it.

Reflection   Talk about how music can affect our mood. Is there a piece of music that always makes you feel sad or always makes you feel happy?

Notes

Sound detector

⑤   ☑ listening
🕐 10 mins   ☑ deduction
🧍 🧍 🧍   ☑ concentration
💬

How to play   The game coordinator walks around the room making sounds on things or
                using objects (e.g. flicking through a book, using chalk on a blackboard).
                Players take turns to wear a blindfold and guess the objects being used.

Adaptations   The whole group keep their eyes closed and try to guess the objects.

                Start with general listening activity – what can you hear in the room? What
                can you hear outside the room? What's the closest sound you can hear?

Reflection   Is listening the same as hearing? When is it hard for you to listen? When is it
                easy? What sounds do you like to listen to? What sounds in the environment
                don't you like?

Notes

Palm painting

⑤

🕐 10 mins

⚕ ⚕ ⚕

💬

☑ taking turns
☑ concentration
☑ trust

How to play   Children work in pairs. One child closes their eyes while the other slowly draws a shape (e.g. circle, square, triangle) or writes a short word on their palm using just one finger. The child who has their eyes closed tries to guess the shape or word. The child who is 'painting' can repeat the pattern up to three times if it is hard to guess. The children then swap places.

Adaptation   One child sits facing away from the group. Players take turns to spell out their name in large letters on this child's back. If the child guesses the name correctly the two swap places.

Reflection   Talk about awareness of touch. Talk about different textures. Which is most sensitive to touch – your back or your fingertips? Are you aware of sensations all the time? For example do you notice your sleeves against your arms all day? Why is it important to be able to change the focus of our attention from one sensation to another or from one task or object to another? Is it possible to pay attention to two different senses or two different tasks at once?

Notes

This and that

⑤   ☑ listening   ☑ observation
🕐 5 mins   ☑ concentration   ☑ self-control
👤 👤 👤
💬

This game is a variation of 'Simon says'.

How to play   The game coordinator demonstrates simple movements for players to follow,
               such as stand on one leg, touch your ear, wave, clap. When the instruction is
               'do this' then players copy the movement. When the instruction is 'do that',
               no one is supposed to move.

Adaptation   Instead of being 'out' when mistakes are made, players continue to join in but
               move to an inner circle. It is likely that all players will be in this circle before
               very long!

Reflection   Talk about self-monitoring and self-awareness. When we repeat something
               often enough we begin not to notice what we are doing. Why is this useful?
               When might it not be useful?

Notes

Guess how!

⑦
🕐 10 mins
🧍 🧍 🧍
💬

☑ listening   ☑ self-monitoring
☑ concentration   ☑ deduction
☑ observation

How to play   Two players leave the room while everyone else decides what 'position' they should take up on their return. This might be something like 'sitting on the floor, facing away from each other with legs outstretched'. The two players return and try to work out how they should be sitting or standing according to how loudly or quietly the other children are clapping. The closer they get to the target position, the louder the other children clap.

Adaptation   The two children who leave the room have to make a 'sculpture' or arrange a series of objects in a certain way chosen by the group.

Reflection   Sometimes we get feedback from others about whether or not we're succeeding in a task or we're 'on the right track', but sometimes we have to rely on our own self-monitoring. Talk about being realistic in self-monitoring. How do you know when you are doing something well? How do you know when you need to do something in a different way?

Notes

Additional notes: more ideas
for self-awareness games

Reflections

14

Wind-downs and celebrations

When you have played several games in a session it is important to have a wind-down activity rather than bringing everything to an abrupt and perhaps unexpected halt. Even if a group has only played one game together it is useful to have a moment of stillness before moving on to the next task for the day. Wind-downs signal to the children that things are coming to a close and allow them preparation time for the ending of the games session.

For on-going groups, small celebrations of talents and achievements should be included at regular intervals. When a group is meeting for the last time it is also vital to make sure that there is opportunity for a longer celebration. This could easily be missed out because of lack of time. It is, however, very important to complete the group in this way. It defines the end of the life of the group as it stands. It gives weight to acknowledging everyone's achievements and it re-enforces the idea that enjoyment and celebration are key ingredients in building self-esteem.

Pack your suitcase

⑧
🕐 5 mins
👤 👤 👤
💬💬

☑ imagination
☑ understanding
  metaphors

☑ dramatic awareness
☑ empathy

How to play   The children are invited to imagine that they each have a suitcase or treasure box that they are going to take away with them when they leave the group. They can choose whatever they want to put into it – perhaps a memory of a particular event or of people in the group, a skill they have developed, a new game that they have learned or something important that someone said to them. Ask each child in turn or ask for volunteers to say what they will pack in their suitcase to take away with them.

Adaptation   Children sit in a circle. Each child takes an imaginary gift from a treasure chest in the centre of the circle and presents it to the person sitting next to them, saying what the gift is and why they are giving it to that person.

Reflection   How will you remind yourself of your achievements? Sometimes we carry heavy suitcases of worries and troubles with us everywhere we go. Try experimenting with carrying *this* suitcase for a while instead!

Notes

Closing circles

⑦
🕐 5 mins
👤 👤 👤
💬💬

☑ listening   ☑ concentration
☑ trust   ☑ self-awareness
☑ taking turns

How to play   At the end of each meeting bring everyone back together again in a circle and finish with each person having the chance to say one brief thing before they leave. For example:

- I feel...

- Today I found out that...

- Today I felt...

- My name is...and I am...

- I have noticed that...

- I feel really good about...

Adaptation   Play a version of 'Feel it, do it' where, instead of saying their name with various emotions, the children do a round of 'I'm brilliant at...' or 'I feel really good about...', expressing the appropriate emotion strongly through body language and facial expression for others to reflect back.

Reflection   Do you set yourself goals to work towards? What would you most like to achieve by the end of next week? Next month? Next term? How will you know when you've achieved it? How will other people know that you've achieved it?

Notes

Big group yell

⑤
🕐 5 mins
👤 👤 👤
💬

☑ listening
☑ cooperation

☑ self-awareness
☑ self-monitoring

How to play   Everyone crouches down together in a huddle. The game coordinator begins a low humming sound and the others join in. As the whole group gradually stands up, the noise level gets louder and louder until everyone jumps into the air and yells as loudly as they can.

Adaptations   Everyone crouches down in a circle facing inwards. Everyone hums quietly and then gradually gets louder as they all stand up together and raise their arms above their heads. Then everyone does the reverse – starting with a loud hum and getting quieter and quieter as they sink down to the ground and eventually they lie down with their feet towards the centre of the circle in complete silence.

Use yogurt-pot shakers to make a crescendo of noise by adding on one person at a time, and then stop one person at a time until there is silence.

Each child makes a noise with something that they have with them – bracelets, crayons, coins, keys. Start slowly, build to a crescendo and then stop one at a time.

Reflection   Talk about beginnings and endings. Talk about sharing experiences in groups and how group games can help us to feel energized and full of confidence.

Notes

Winning the Oscars

ⓖ
🕐 10 mins
🚶 🚶 🚶
🗨

☑ self-confidence
☑ trust
☑ imagination

☑ giving and receiving praise
☑ dramatic awareness

How to play — Cover a wooden spoon or an artist's figure with tin foil. Present this to each child in turn at an imaginary 'award ceremony' for whatever he or she would most like to have an award for. This could be a past achievement, a future goal or something completely fantastical. Really over-play their achievement. The whole group celebrate each award with plenty of clapping and cheering, etc.

Adaptation — Players take turns to be a 'national treasure'. The rest of the group take turns to walk up to this person and shake hands or give words of praise or thanks.

Reflection — Talk about the importance of noticing and celebrating our real achievements and sometimes giving ourselves a verbal or an actual reward for our hard work. Think of small ways that we can reward ourselves and reward others, e.g. make Dad a cup of tea, clean Jim's bike for him, pat someone on the back, invite friends round for a game of football.

Notes

Pirate's treasure parachute game

⑤   ☑ listening   ☑ empathy
🕐 10 mins   ☑ cooperation   ☑ trust
👤 👤 👤
💬

How to play   Everyone puts one possession in a 'treasure' box. Put the box under the parachute. Players hold the parachute at waist level and make 'waves'. Divers take turns to go under the waves to gather one piece of treasure and return it to its owner.

Adaptation   Retrieve treasure according to different qualities or shape, e.g. find something wooden, find something made of metal, find something round.

Reflection   Our talents, abilities, personality characteristics and ideas are all examples of our personal 'treasure'. Do you know what is in your treasure box? Make a list of things that you would like other people to know about you.

Notes

Additional notes: more ideas for wind-downs and celebrations

Reflections

Examples of different types of games

Competitive/non-competitive games

Active/stationary

Word games

Sound games

Silent games

Movement games

Mathematical games

Board games

Sports/team games – small, large, pairs

Outdoor/indoor

Structured/non-structured

Eyes closed/eyes open

Small space/big space

Logical

Street games

Quizzes

Card games

Computer games

Props/no props

Seasonal

Energizing/calming

Risk taking/safe

Themed

Challenging/difficult

Subject index

Author index

Acknowledgements

The idea for this book was conceived by Stephen Jones, commissioning editor at Jessica Kingsley Publishers, and nurtured through its various stages by project editor Lyndsey Dodd. The games themselves have been collected during more than 20 years of practice as a speech and language therapist and as a workshop facilitator. A handful have come from resource books and of these, I have found books by Mildred Masheder, Barbara Sher and by Donna Brandes and Howard Phillips (*Gamesters' Handbook*) the most useful. For the majority of the games however I am unable to acknowledge original sources – some will undoubtedly be familiar to readers as versions of traditional party games, others were passed on to me by children, therapists, students and teachers during therapy and training courses. I can therefore only say an all inclusive 'thank you' to the many game-players who so enthusiastically keep the tradition of children's games alive in all its diversity and who have been kind enough to share their favourites with me over the years.

Lightning Source UK Ltd.
Milton Keynes UK
UKOW05f1523120516

274103UK00001B/4/P